# Using Program Theory
# in Evaluation

Leonard Bickman, *Editor*
*Vanderbilt University*

**NEW DIRECTIONS FOR PROGRAM EVALUATION**
A Publication of the American Evaluation Association
*A joint organization of the Evaluation Research Society
and the Evaluation Network*
MARK W. LIPSEY, *Editor-in-Chief*
*Claremont Graduate School*

Number 33, Spring 1987

Paperback sourcebooks in
The Jossey-Bass Higher Education and
Social and Behavioral Sciences Series

Jossey-Bass Inc., Publishers
San Francisco • London

Leonard Bickman (ed.).
*Using Program Theory in Evaluation.*
New Directions for Program Evaluation, no. 33.
San Francisco: Jossey-Bass, 1987.

*New Directions for Program Evaluation Series*
A publication of the American Evaluation Association
Mark W. Lipsey, *Editor-in-Chief*

*New Directions for Program Evaluation* is published quarterly by
Jossey-Bass Inc., Publishers (publication number USPS 449-050),
and is sponsored by the American Evaluation Association.
Second-class postage rates are paid at San Francisco, California, and at
additional mailing offices. POSTMASTER: Send address changes to
Jossey-Bass Inc., Publishers, 433 California Street, San Francisco,
California 94104.

**Editorial correspondence** should be sent to the Editor-in-Chief,
Mark Lipsey, Psychology Department, Claremont Graduate School,
Claremont, Calif. 91711.

Library of Congress Catalog Card Number LC 85-644749

International Standard Serial Number ISSN 0164-7989

International Standard Book Number ISBN 1-55542-968-8

Cover art by WILLI BAUM

Manufactured in the United States of America

# Ordering Information

The paperback sourcebooks listed below are published quarterly and can be ordered either by subscription or single copy.

Subscriptions cost $52.00 per year for institutions, agencies, and libraries. Individuals can subscribe at the special rate of $39.00 per year *if payment is by personal check.* (Note that the full rate of $52.00 applies if payment is by institutional check, even if the subscription is designated for an individual.) Standing orders are accepted.

Single copies are available at $12.95 when payment accompanies order. (California, New Jersey, New York, and Washington, D.C., residents please include appropriate sales tax.) For billed orders, cost per copy is $12.95 plus postage and handling.

Substantial discounts are offered to organizations and individuals wishing to purchase bulk quantities of Jossey-Bass sourcebooks. Please inquire.

Please note that these prices are for the academic year 1986–1987 and are subject to change without prior notice. Also, some titles may be out of print and therefore not available for sale.

To ensure correct and prompt delivery, all orders must give either the *name of an individual* or an *official purchase order number.* Please submit your order as follows:

*Subscriptions:* specify series and year subscription is to begin.
*Single Copies:* specify sourcebook code (such as, PE1) and first two words of title.

Mail orders for United States and Possessions, Latin America, Canada, Japan, Australia, and New Zealand to:
Jossey-Bass Inc., Publishers
433 California Street
San Francisco, California 94104

Mail orders for all other parts of the world to:
Jossey-Bass Limited
28 Banner Street
London EC1Y 8QE

## New Directions for Program Evaluation Series
Mark W. Lipsey, *Editor-in-Chief*

PE1 *Exploring Purposes and Dimensions,* Scarvia B. Anderson, Claire D. Coles
PE2 *Evaluating Federally Sponsored Programs,* Charlotte C. Rentz, R. Robert Rentz
PE3 *Monitoring Ongoing Programs,* Donald L. Grant

PE4     *Secondary Analysis*, Robert F. Boruch

PE5     *Utilization of Evaluative Information*, Larry A. Braskamp, Robert D. Brown

PE6     *Measuring the Hard-to-Measure*, Edward H. Loveland

PE7     *Values, Ethics, and Standards in Evaluation*, Robert Perloff, Evelyn Perloff

PE8     *Training Program Evaluators*, Lee Sechrest

PE9     *Assessing and Interpreting Outcomes*, Samuel Ball

PE10    *Evaluation of Complex Systems*, Ronald J. Wooldridge

PE11    *Measuring Effectiveness*, Dan Baugher

PE12    *Federal Efforts to Develop New Evaluation Methods*, Nick L. Smith

PE13    *Field Assessments of Innovative Evaluation Methods*, Nick L. Smith

PE14    *Making Evaluation Research Useful to Congress*, Leonard Saxe, Daniel Koretz

PE15    *Standards for Evaluation Practice*, Peter H. Rossi

PE16    *Applications of Time Series Analysis to Evaluation*, Garlie A. Forehand

PE17    *Stakeholder-Based Evaluation*, Anthony S. Bryk

PE18    *Management and Organization of Program Evaluation*, Robert G. St. Pierre

PE19    *Philosophy of Evaluation*, Ernest R. House

PE20    *Developing Effective Internal Evaluation*, Arnold J. Love

PE21    *Making Effective Use of Mailed Questionnaires*, Daniel C. Lockhart

PE22    *Secondary Analysis of Available Data Bases*, David J. Bowering

PE23    *Evaluating the New Information Technologies*, Jerome Johnston

PE24    *Issues in Data Synthesis*, William H. Yeaton, Paul M. Wortman

PE25    *Culture and Evaluation*, Michael Quinn Patton

PE26    *Economic Evaluations of Public Programs*, James S. Catterall

PE27    *Utilizing Prior Research in Evaluation Planning*, David S. Cordray

PE28    *Randomization and Field Experimentation*, Robert F. Boruch, Werner Wothke

PE29    *Teaching of Evaluation Across the Disciplines*, Barbara Gross Davis

PE30    *Naturalistic Evaluation*, David D. Williams

PE31    *Advances in Quasi-Experimental Design and Analysis*, William M. K. Trochim

PE32    *Measuring Efficiency: An Assessment of Data Envelopment Analysis*, Richard H. Silkman

# Contents

**Editor's Notes**                                                                    1
Leonard Bickman

**1. The Functions of Program Theory**                                                 5
Leonard Bickman
Program theory can improve evaluation's contribution to social science
knowledge, clarify the problem, and improve consensus formation.

**2. Measuring and Testing Program Philosophy**                                       19
Kendon J. Conrad, Todd Q. Miller
The concept of program theory is expanded by including values and
methods for measuring them.

**3. Conceptual and Action Heuristics: Tools for the Evaluator**                      43
Charles McClintock
A set of techniques to improve both programs and policies is described.

**4. Program Theory and Implementation Theory:**                                      59
**Implications for Evaluators**
Mary Ann Scheirer
Program theory is linked to implementation theory to improve compre-
hensiveness of evaluations.

**5. Evaluability Assessment: Developing Program Theory**                             77
Joseph S. Wholey
Evaluability assessment is applied to measure program theory.

**6. Program Micro- and Macrotheories: A Guide for**                                  93
**Social Change**
William R. Shadish, Jr.
Program theory is not only important in understanding the effects of pro-
grams but also in effecting change outside of programs.

**Index**                                                                           111

# New Directions for Program Evaluation

A Quarterly Publication of the American Evaluation Association
(A Joint Organization of the Evaluation Research Society and the
Evaluation Network)

*American Evaluation Association, 9555 Persimmon Tree Road, Potomac, MD 20854*

# Editor's Notes

Evaluation is often referred to as a practical science, but both as a practice and as a science it requires theory. Although there are a variety of theoretical approaches to the conduct of evaluation, there has yet to be serious consideration of the relationship between the evaluation itself and the theoretical underpinnings of the program. All too often evaluators focus on the technical aspects of the evaluation process (design and measurement) and pay scant attention to the program. A successful evaluation can produce some short-term results and possibly local change, but without considering the theory underlying the program, neither evaluators, program developers, nor program implementors can hope to produce generalizable findings. This volume describes the need for program theory in planning and conducting evaluations and provides a variety of approaches for understanding and measuring program theory.

In the first chapter I review ten positive functions of program theory. Program theory is necessary to improve evaluation's contribution to social science knowledge as well as to assist policymakers in understanding how programs work. A good program theory can aid work with stakeholders and the development of appropriate measurement procedures. These and other functions support the argument for more emphasis on program theory in evaluation.

In the second chapter Conrad and Miller review the short history of program theory in evaluation to support their belief that program philosophy is important. They attempt to go beyond the simple question of Did it work? They point out that program philosophy (the combination of theory and values) determines the way in which programs meet client needs. These philosophies link causes and effects. The authors show how conceptual maps measure program philosophy among key stakeholders. They further show how this procedure can clarify goals, assist in the measurement of implementation, and clearly relate outcomes to goals.

Program theory can also be used to improve programs and policies. Drawing from literature on measurement and evaluation, organizational behavior, and development and learning theory, McClintock in Chapter Three describes techniques that can expand conceptions of problems and solutions and can also focus on specific alternatives for action. These guides, or heuristics, can be used to expand thinking about concepts and their interrelationships. In addition to these conceptual development tools, it is necessary to provide methods useful in the real world of program decision making. These tools include the use of metaphors, structural

1

processes for clarifying concepts, and mapping. These techniques can create a better understanding of the complexity underlying both social problems and programs.

Program theory can and should guide implementation. The relationship between theory and implementation provides the basis for judging program fidelity. Without a clear and explicit theory and without a process for measuring implementation, it is impossible to determine if the appropriate treatment was delivered. In Chapter Four, Scheirer goes a step further and describes the relationship between program theory and implementation theory. The former describes the set of cause-and-effect relationships, and the latter provides an understanding of why a program is delivered as it is. Scheirer describes the types of data that can inform both theories and the way they contribute to better and more comprehensive evaluations. Scheirer attempts to shift evaluators' roles from simply measuring program outcomes to the necessity of describing the program as designed (theory) and its actual implementation.

Evaluability assessment can be used to judge whether a program can be evaluated. When the procedure is competently applied, it can help the evaluator determine if the definition of the program is clearly addressed, if there are testable assumptions linking program input to outcome, and if there is agreement on priorities of evaluation and its application. In Chapter Five, Wholey uses evaluability assessment procedures to identify program theory and involve key policymakers and staff. Evaluability assessment is another well-developed process that can be used to clarify program theory.

In the last chapter Shadish amplifies on the two uses of the term *program theory*. Up to this point, all authors have used the term to describe the model of the program, a use which Shadish calls microtheory. His chapter on program macrotheory is concerned with factors that affect change. Shadish explores program theory in the context of social change. He indicates the barriers to successful utilization of evaluation and suggests ways to overcome them. Some of these solutions require evaluators to make often hard and unpopular decisions. Theory development relevant to program changes must be further articulated if evaluators are to make significant, long-lasting contributions to society. Program macrotheory is one way of enabling evaluators to make such contributions.

These chapters provide a conceptualization of program theory that requires more emphasis in program evaluation and also provide the means to measure program theory. These tools will require further work but, with the conceptual perspectives, will provide the evaluator with the necessary information to incorporate program theory in evaluations.

Leonard Bickman
Editor

*Leonard Bickman is professor of psychology at Peabody College, Vanderbilt University. He is director of the Program Evaluation Laboratory at Peabody and director of the Center for Mental Health Policy at the Vanderbilt Institute for Public Policy Studies.*

*The role of theory in program evaluation is an important
but neglected area in evaluation practice and theory.
Program theory has several important functions that can
improve our ability to generalize from particular evaluations,
contribute to social science theory, and achieve consensus in
evaluation planning.*

# The Functions of
# Program Theory

*Leonard Bickman*

## A Definition of Program Theory

Program theory, as defined in this chapter, is the construction of a
plausible and sensible model of how a progam is supposed to work. Typically these models are developed for a particular program and do not
represent "off-the-shelf" use of a single established social science theory.
The other authors in this volume also provide definitions of program
theory. Conrad uses the term *program philosophy* to describe a system of
beliefs, values, and goals that define the structure, process, and outcomes
of a program. Scheirer indicates that program theory clarifies the set of
cause-and-effect relationships and thus provides the rationale for the treatment. She further elaborates on the differences between program theory
and implementation theory. Program theory according to McClintock
includes scientific explanations, implicit theories, models of inputs, processes, and outputs, as well as policy statements. McClintock concentrates
in his chapter on understanding the role of implicit theories. Wholey
defines the functions of program theory as the identification of resources,
activities, and outcomes of a program and the causal assumptions that
connect these. Shadish divides program theory into program macrotheory
and microtheory. Microtheory provides a description of the program being

L. Bickman (ed.). *Using Program Theory in Evaluation.*
New Directions for Program Evaluation, no. 33. San Francisco: Jossey-Bass, Spring 1987.

evaluated, while macrotheory is concerned primarily with social change. Shadish notes that the microtheory approach is taken by a number of theorists (Bickman, 1985a; Chen and Rossi, 1981, 1983; Cronbach, 1982; Stake, 1978; Wholey, 1977). While Shadish tends to emphasize the macrotheory level in his discussion, the other authors focus on the microtheory perspective. The microtheory will be the focus of this chapter—that is, the concern for describing the logic of the program (how the program is supposed to affect the problem).

Theory tends to be an overused word, and in a sense we may be contributing to this overuse. The term *theory* as used by program developers and implementors typically is used to mean a vague notion or hunch not usually based on social science information. Often the objectives, goals, and theory underlying the program may be purposely ambiguous because of political concerns; that is, it may be kept intentionally vague in order to gain support from different groups. Moreover, developers and implementors often do not have in-depth training in theories of behavior. These factors all contribute to the too-common fact that programs lack explicit theory or that the theory espoused may be implausible. Thus we can expect that program theory, as typically stated by program developers, may be nothing more than a few simple assumptions about why the program should work. Evaluators must develop a more elaborate causal network that describes the bases of the program instead of relying on intuition and assumption.

This is not to imply that there is only one correct program theory. Different theories may be applied depending on the discipline of the evaluator. A psychologist may prefer to develop a program theory using individual cognitions and attitudes as a basis, while a sociologist may prefer to use roles and organizational variables. An economist will probably be most comfortable using a microeconomic theory. Different theories at the same level of analysis can also be developed by using different sets of explanatory variables. One evaluator studying a program designed to improve schools might focus on the teacher's motivations to improve, while another investigator might develop a theory that relates school improvement to changes in relationships between teachers. It is important to develop not necessarily the best program theory but *a* program theory. This implies that different constructs may equally account for program effects. This is not surprising, since programs are rarely developed to test a single theory. The theory-based evaluation can confirm a particular program theory but usually cannot determine if other program theories are invalid.

## The Functions of Program Theory

Program evaluation has progressed in the last twenty years from applying the simple input/output, or black-box, model of evaluation to moving "inside" the box to try to understand what goes on in the program (Cook and Shadish, 1986). There are a number of benefits that accrue to an evaluation that has a clear program theory.

*Contributing to Social Science Knowledge.* Evaluation can be an important source of social science data (Chen and Rossi, 1981). Social science theory evolves from a variety of inputs. One important source is studies in which an investigator intervenes in a situation to determine the effects of that intervention. For example, most social psychological experiments are derived from laboratory experiments in which the researcher manipulates a theoretically meaningful independent variable to determine its effect on a theoretically meaningful dependent variable. The key to the study's theoretical contribution is in the theoretical relevance of the independent and dependent variables. In Campbell's terminology this is described as a construct of cause validity and a construct of effect validity (Cook and Campbell, 1979). That is, both the independent and dependent variables must be demonstrated to be good operationalizations of higher order and more abstract constructs. A classic example of poor construct validity is found in older studies dealing with aggression. The number of times a child knocked down a bobo doll was often used to indicate level of aggression even though there was little evidence to link this to more meaningful aggressive behavior (Bandura, 1973). Later studies indicated that this measure was not a good operationalization of aggression.

Program evaluation can make important contributions to social science theory if the program (independent variable) and measures of program process and outcome (dependent variables) are theoretically meaningful. These variables are theoretically meaningful if they are high in construct validity. We as evaluators can help ensure good construct validity by developing sound program theory. An example from some of my own work may help illustrate this.

One of my current projects involves examining the effects of offering schools a financial incentive to improve instruction (Bickman, 1985b). Approximately ninety schools were randomly assigned to a control and a treatment condition. In the latter condition schools were informed that they would be eligible to receive up to $1,000 per teacher if they improved their achievement test scores. As a policy experiment the data should prove very useful to those considering such a program. But because of the theoretical meaningfulness of the study, a program theory was developed to explain how the incentive may operate. The model developed includes both school level organizational variables and teacher and principal individual level data. The model was designed to assist the evaluators in understanding why the intervention did or did not work, which thus added to knowledge about how schools improve their performance.

Our concern to contribute to social science theory resulted in two important features of the evaluation. First, a theoretical perspective was developed that related the incentive to teacher attitudes and behaviors and school context variables. Second, measures were developed and data were collected that tested this model. If incentives operate as we think they do, then we will have contributed to social science knowledge about teacher motivation and organizational change. Moreover, even if the incentive has no effect, we will have created a theoretically meaningful data base that includes attitudes and perceptions of over 1,300 teachers and principals collected longitudinally over a four-year period and that is linked to student achievement data. We are not aware of another data base in education that is similar to this one. When asked by the executive director of the foundation that funded this project whether we could fail, our response was no, because even if the incentive does not work, we will still learn a great deal about how schools operate. To accomplish this understanding we needed to develop a theory of how the program would work.

In this project the program microtheory can produce knowledge that can be used to build and test theories dealing with clients (students), staff (teachers and principals), and organizational characteristics (schools). Other studies can be designed to add to our knowledge about cost, effects, and impacts. Program evaluation can then serve as a rigorous and valid test of a social science theoretical perspective. This is only possible when the theoretical implications have been thought out and implemented in the program and appropriate data has been collected by the evaluators.

*Assisting Policymakers.* The social science contribution of evaluation may be of most interest to academic evaluators. The academic may feel comfortable about adding to the fund of knowledge about a social phenomena. A case can also be made that social policymakers should be interested in programs that incorporate social theories (Cronbach, 1982). The ability to generalize from a specific evaluation is also significant for policymakers. They need to know whether the results of a particular program indicate that the program or some aspects of the program will work in some other setting and time.

The ability to understand the constructs underlying the program should help the policymaker know if different operationalizations of the program will work in a fashion similar to the program that was evaluated. Although generalizing the effects of a program to different populations, times, or locations is a major concern of policymakers, another form of generalizability is the ability to infer that different operational definitions of the program theory would also produce similar effects. This is a contrast between external validity and construct of cause validity (Cook and Campbell, 1979). Construct of cause validity means relating a particular intervention to a larger set of interventions than the one evaluated exemplifies. This process of connection is inferential and requires that certain elements in the program be matched to the elements in the theory (Cook, Leviton, and Shadish, 1985). In the parlance of experimentation, the program is an operationalization of the construct or concept underlying the program. Conceptualizing the program as a complex set of independent variables that refer to a broader and even more complex set of variables (the construct) demonstrates the relevance of program theory to construct generalization.

Without being able to specify these theory elements, it cannot be determined if a particular program is a valid operationalization of the theory underlying the program. The nature of the generalizability process requires not only that the nature of the program be explicated but also the nature of the theory underlying the program be explicated. Only then is it possible to tell if the particular program is a good representation of the theory.

It is important for policymakers to know just how far the design implementation of a particular intervention can depart from the intervention theory before that intervention appears to be based on some other, possible unproven theory. For example, if the theory underlying an intervention to improve student achievement is based on increasing teacher efficacy, then there may be a variety of acceptable interventions that can be theoretically linked to increasing teacher efficacy. Local options may include different interventions that all could be valid operationalizations of a theory that linked teacher efficacy to student achievement. Knowledge of which interventions are valid and which are not requires a clearly defined theory of how teacher efficacy affects student achievement. Sites should be permitted, and perhaps encouraged, to try different types of interventions as long as they validly reflect the program theory under consideration. By using different interventions both the policy and the research community can be informed about the robustness of the theory.

For example, a theory linking teacher efficacy to student performance might include a variety of ways of increasing efficacy. Such interventions that provide the teacher with feedback about how well the teacher was teaching or with small experiences of students' success might increase the teacher's sense of competence and effectiveness. However, increasing the quality of the curriculum would not be included as an intervention that could affect efficacy. Thus, having demonstrated a linkage between various ways of affecting efficacy and its impact on achievement, both the theoretician and policymaker are better prepared to address the limits of the theory and its application.

The policymaker must know if the multiple ways a program was implemented at different sites provide similar feedback on validity of the program. A clearly articulated program theory allows the policymaker to determine if the different implementations are simple variations of the same construct or are different constructs. For example, in a statewide evaluation of preschool programs (Bickman and Rog, 1986), policymakers wished to know what types of programs were effective. A typology of program components was developed to provide a partial answer to this question (Bickman, 1985a). Policymakers now had a program theory to help them make funding decisions.

By examining the model that links the components of programs to specific program sites, policymakers could use this information in deciding if a particular site was effective or if that model of intervention was working. By being able to discriminate between these two perspectives, policymakers could withdraw support from certain types of program components or take corrective action at particular sites if the component model was effective but was not being properly implemented. Moreover, state policy could be charged to provide statewide support for components that appeared to be both theoretically sound and properly implemented at a variety of sites.

This abstract analysis does not, at this point, reflect whether the actual implementation of the program is a good representation of the theory. This difference is discussed by Scheirer (this volume). First, we need to know if the program as designed is a good representation of the program theory.

***Discriminating Between Program Failure and Theory Failure.*** Suchman (1967) and Weiss (1972) describe a clear relationship between program failure and theory failure. This distinction indicates that failure to find program effects can be due either to the wrong theory or the program not being properly implemented. A third cause of failure can be due to a faulty evaluation design. Design, measurement, and statistical power problems could produce a Type II error; that is, finding no difference when in fact the program was effective. In planning an evaluation the evaluator must be able to defend the design, measurement, and statistical analysis so that if a no-effect finding is obtained, the basis for this finding is not considered the evaluator's fault.

For example, an evaluation of a school health program indicated no change in student attitudes or behaviors. The program director claimed that the reason no effect was found was because the evaluator used insensitive measures. However, the evaluator was able to show through a number of subsidiary studies that the measurement of attitude and behavior was very sensitive to small experimental manipulations (Edwards, Hotch, and Bickman, 1982). Similarly, Lipsey and others (1985) show that many of the evaluations they studied did not have sufficient statistical power to detect small differences that would be expected from the program. Sixty percent of the studies did not have sufficient statistical power for medium size effects. Thus, the first question that should be raised is whether or not the evaluation was sufficiently well designed to detect any meaningful effects that might be present.

The second point raised by Weiss (1972) concerns implementation of the program. Scheirer (this volume) points out the important relationships between program theory and implementation. Program theory failure cannot be distinguished from program implementation failure unless there is evidence that the program was implemented with fidelity.

Finally, if there is evidence that the evaluation plan was successfully implemented and the program was implemented with integrity, only then can the evaluation be considered a test of the program theory. Evaluated under sensitive conditions and implemented with fidelity, does the program produce the intended effects? If it does not, the validity of the theory underlying the program can be questioned. If the necessary conditions were met and the program produced no effect, it might be appropriate to discard the theory underlying the program.

The conditions set for testing the program theory may not be present, yet null effects may be ascribed to theory failure. The literature is replete with examples of interventions that are considered not to work when in fact the intervention was never really attempted. The use of wrong or insensitive measures or of poorly implemented programs (Scheirer, 1981) does not provide optimal conditions for testing theories.

*Identifying the Problem and Target Group.* A program theory should also be able to clarify the relationship between the program and the problem. A program is typically designed to solve some problem for a targeted group. It is assumed that if the program is implemented properly it will affect the problem afflicting the group. Program implementors and developers may not carefully spell out such a relationship. A program may be implemented with a group or for a problem for which it is inappropriate.

Rog and Bickman (1984) report such an evaluation. In their feedback-research approach to evaluation, they point out that implementation failure may not be caused by failure to follow procedures but by failure to apply the program to the appropriate target. In their example a stress management program for employees was implemented based on the assumption that the source of stress was at home. A theoretically sound program was designed to teach employees how to deal with stress at home. Data collected during the evaluation indicated that the employees were not experiencing stress at home but were experiencing it on the job. Thus, this was not a good test of the theory underlying the program, since there was no problem-program match. A well-articulated program theory should spell out the conditions under which the program would produce positive effects. Clearly articulating the nature of the problem and the group affected is part of the program theory.

*Providing Program Implementation Description.* Scheirer (this volume) provides an excellent description of the relationship between implementation theory and program theory. A good program theory will describe the elements and components of a program. Bickman (1985a) provides a procedure for developing a description of program components. This description should be included in the program theory. However, more than just describing the elements or components of a program is necessary; the theory must also specify the relative importance of these elements.

To determine if there is a good implementation of the program, the critical components of the program to be implemented must be known in order to adequately test the theory. The most basic question to ask the program director is "What aspects of the program, if left out, would doom the program to failure?" The difficulty of describing a complex program and answering this question is part of the problem of doing good implementation analysis. Programs are not simple variables. They are complex elements and components that are not independent of each other. Thus, it is a major task to indicate which are the most critical components. A clearly articulated program theory assists in making these judgments. It informs the evaluator which activities, among the many implemented by a program, the evaluator must be able to assess.

*Uncovering Unintended Effects.* One of the advantages of describing a program theory is being able to go beyond the objectives specified by project staff. According to Scriven's (1980) goal-free philosophy, theory construction and development allows the evaluator to look for either positive or negative effects where they might not be expected by program designers and implementors. The underlying theory allows the evaluator to depart from political objectives and instead focus on objectives that can be inferred from the operation of the theory.

*Specifying Intervening Variables.* Program theory by definition provides causal links between the operation of the program and its intended effects. In developing such a theory, a schematic presentation of those links is feasible. Linkages move from the operations of the programs to intervening proximal and distal variables. The theory specifies how the program activities relate to the ultimate outcomes of the project. Weiss (1972) terms some intervening variables *bridging variables,* since they link the inputs of the program to its ultimate outcomes. Bridging variables are often derived from the subgoals of the program. Bickman (1983) describes a process, or flow model, approach that is typically developed as part of an evaluability assessment (Rutman, 1980; Wholey, 1977). This flowchart approach visually connects program inputs (activities) with proximal and distal goals. Ways to develop this approach are described by McClintock (this volume) and Wholey (this volume).

*Improving Formative Use of Evaluation.* Program theory can specify the intermediate effects of a program before it has manifested its ultimate effects. For example, if a program is designed to change a person's eating habits, a theoretical approach may specify that the person must know which foods are appropriate to eat. Thus, knowledge of appropriate foods would be an intermediate goal. A black-box evaluation would not measure the participant's knowledge, but a theory-based approach should provide such measurement. If in the early stages of the program the evaluation indicates that people are not learning which foods are appropriate, it would be pointless to examine dietary behavior. Armed with this knowledge, the evaluator could inform the program personnel that they must introduce an educational component into the program. Thus, by theoretically describing the effects and assumptions of the program, the evaluator can often provide corrective action for a program implementor.

*Clarifying Measurement Issues.* The theoretical perspective allows the evaluator to develop and choose measures that are valid for the program. Without theory, it is not clear to the evaluator which measures must be used or the validity of these measures. A classic example of this problem is the evaluation of the early Head Start studies. Apparently, IQ tests were used because they were considered reliable, valid measures, although from the program developer's perspective, they were not relevant to the predicted outcomes. A clear theoretical statement about the outcomes that could be expected from the interventions developed would have led the evaluators to choose other instruments. Without this theoretical structure, it is difficult for the evaluator to know whether measurements are validly related to the program.

*Improving Consensus Formation.* Wholey (this volume) and Conrad (this volume) point out that the perspectives of stakeholders are often important considerations in developing an evaluation. However, previous work on stakeholders has not focused on the stakeholders' perceptions of program theory but on more practical questions of acceptability of measures and research design. Both Wholey and Conrad point out that the stakeholder's implicit theory of the program may in fact be an important underlying construct that should be studied. The evaluator should not assume full responsibility of designing a program theory. The process of developing program theory may be more informative and educational for stakeholders in helping them understand the limits of the program than any other procedure. This understanding may lead to more realistic expectations.

## The Development of Program Theory

It would seem self-evident to develop the program theory before the program is implemented. Moreover, persons who are professionally trained to develop programs should be responsible for theory development. However, as many evaluators know from experience, both circumstances are relatively rare. Programs seem to grow from notions and ideas. The program may be developed and implemented by individuals who have no training in traditional social science terminology and rationale. Thus, the evaluator often must develop the theory in order to address measurement and design issues. The theory must be developed to create a valid measurement and design plan. The evaluator must make decisions about what variables must be measured and how they should be measured.

It is rare that a program document theoretically describes the relationships between program activities and various levels of outcomes. In an earlier paper, Bickman (1979) notes that an important contribution social psychologists could make to social action is to develop good theories of programs, rather than just apply sophisticated methodologies. The psychologist, armed with knowledge of human behavior, should be especially well suited for developing theoretically sound and effective models of interventions.

*Program Theory: From Implicit to Explicit.* Every program has a theory. Unfortunately, it may be implicit, fragmented, and not well conceptualized. These theories are composed of a number of important assumptions that can include basic constructs such as human nature, assumptions about the nature of the problem and of the population, and the boundary, or limiting conditions, of the effects of the program. These assumptions are in addition to assumptions about the causal linkages within the program. Chen and Rossi (1983) indicate that "often enough policymakers and program designers are not social scientists, and their theories (if any) are likely to be simply the current folklore of the upper-middle-brow media" (p. 285). Chen and Rossi go on to note that social science theories may be in direct opposition to the working assumptions of policymakers. But can these implicit theories simply be ignored? The existence of implicit theory can have ramifications for the conduct and utilization of an evaluation. An evaluation that is designed to test a theory contrary to the implicit theory of the major stakeholders can create problems when the evaluation is implemented and the results of the evaluation are utilized. The design of an evaluation can vary according to the program theory used. Depending on the assumptions made, more than one theory can be developed to examine the effects of a program.

Basic social psychological research on decision making and social theories (Anderson and Sechler, 1986; Janis and Mann, 1977; Lord, Ross, and Lepper, 1979; Shaklee and Fischoff, 1982) indicates that the social theories people have about events are in a large part based on causal explanations of how social variables interrelate. There is some evidence (Lord, Ross, and Lepper, 1979) that people who have extreme beliefs about the causal nature of social events are not only biased in how they interpret new information but become more polarized when exposed to information that contradicts their initial theory.

These studies imply that the initial causal beliefs of key stakeholders can affect their cooperation in implementing an evaluation and their reactions to evaluation findings that do not fit their initial theory of the program. It thus becomes important to discover what implicit theories stakeholders have about the program being evaluated.

There are a number of techniques described in this volume that attempt to make the implicit theory explicit. Wholey uses evaluability assessment procedures to discover the implicit theories held by stakeholders. These procedures include the construction of logic models and repeated meetings with policymakers to obtain their concurrence with the model. McClintock uses conceptual heuristics that allow the investigator to clarify and map the subjective theories held by stakeholders. Conrad and Miller employ questionnaires to uncover the program's causal model.

There are, of course, other techniques that can be used. Weick and Bougon (1986) describe procedures to develop cognitive maps that they use to describe causal theories of respondents. This procedure allows respondents to use their own language to describe how they understand issues and relationships. Evaluators can also use sorting techniques (Canter, Brown, and Groat, 1985) and intensive interviewing methods (Brenner, 1985) to discover implicit theories. Many of these procedures are exploratory; however, they are potentially an effective and objective means to make implicit theories explicit.

*Theory in Use.* One of the few studies that has examined the use of program theory in evaluation was conducted by Lipsey and others (1985). Lipsey and his colleagues examined 119 evaluation studies and divided them into nontheoretical, subtheoretical, and theoretical categories. These categories were designed to discriminate among different levels of theoretical sophistication. At the lowest level were nontheoretical descriptions of the program wherein little or no information on the program was provided other than of a simple, descriptive nature. These descriptions could be called black-box evaluations. At the subtheoretical level Lipsey and others categorized evaluations into either descriptions of the program strategy (operation or service goals with little or no reference to outcomes) or of the program principles (in these the evaluation provided general statements about the treatment but no information about the relationship between the treatment and the expected outcomes). Two levels of theoretical descriptions were also used. The first one, hypothesis testing, was used when programs attempted to relate elements to specified outcomes. These were typically very limited, ad hoc explanations and were not generalizable. The second level, integrated theory, provided an a priori theory within which program elements, rationale, and causal linkages were described. (An example of the latter is the use of social learning theory in a program that provided assertiveness training for battered spouses.)

When these classifications were applied to the 119 evaluation studies, it was found that about two-thirds of the sample had no theoretical basis higher than subtheoretical. Only about 9 percent of the studies displayed integrated theories, while about 20 percent were of the nontheoretical, black-box variety. Interestingly, neither the academic affiliation of the author nor the program area had any relation to the level of program theory in the study. Thus, the level of sophistication of evaluators in providing a theoretical description of the program under study is somewhat disappointing. However, the poor use of program theory in evaluation is not exceptional in otherwise well-designed evaluations. Lipsey and others found equally dismal findings when examining measurement, design, and statistical power.

Not all evaluation theorists emphasize the positive use of program theory. As Cook and Shadish (1986) point out, both Campbell and Scriven emphasize "identifying manipulable solutions" over "identifying generalizable explanations" (p. 225). Campbell's (1969) experimenting society and Scriven's (1983) consumer model of evaluation represent this point of view. Cook and Shadish (1986) note that this approach to evaluation, which dominated the beginning of evaluation, is now declining but they caution that much of value will be lost if this declining perspective is completely dismissed.

## Summary

Program theory is an important but neglected aspect of program evaluation. Although its importance was recognized early in the history of evaluation, it has not received much attention in the literature until recently, and in practice it has received even less attention. This is surprising given the positive functions program theory has in program evaluation. In this chapter we have noted ten functions program theory can have, as follows:

- Contributing to social science knowledge
- Assisting policymakers
- Discriminating between theory failure and program failure
- Identifying the problem and target group
- Providing program implementation description
- Uncovering unintended effects
- Specifying intervening variables
- Improving formative use of evaluation
- Clarifying measurement issues
- Improving consensus formation.

Many programs are not developed with a strong and coherent theory, but instead the theory underlying the program must often be developed by the program evaluator in an attempt to perform some of the measurement and design tasks. Finally, program theory is used in a small proportion of reported evaluations.

## References

Anderson, C. A., and Sechler, E. S. "Effects Explanation and Counterexplanation in the Development and Use of Social Theories." *Journal of Personality and Social Psychology*, 1986, *50*, 24–34.

Bandura, A. *Aggression: A Social Learning Analysis.* Englewood Cliffs, N.J.: Prentice-Hall, 1973.

Bickman, L. "Program Evaluation and Social Psychology: The Achievement of Relevancy." *Personality and Social Psychology Bulletin,* 1979, *5,* 483-490.

Bickman, L. "Evaluating Prevention Programs." *Journal of Social Issues,* 1983, *39,* 181.

Bickman, L. "Improving Established Statewide Programs: A Component Theory of Evaluation." *Evaluation Review,* 1985a, *9,* 189-208.

Bickman, L. "Randomized Field Experiments in Education: Implementation Lessons." In R. Boruch and W. Wothke (eds.), *Randomization and Field Experimentation.* New Directions for Program Evaluation, no. 28. San Francisco: Jossey-Bass, 1985b.

Bickman, L., and Rog, D. "The Use of Stakeholders in Planning Evaluations of Early Intervention Programs." In L. Bickman and D. Weatherford (eds.), *Evaluating Early Intervention Programs for Severely Handicapped Children and Their Families.* Austin, Tex.: Pro-ed Press, 1986.

Brenner, M. "Intensive Interviewing." In M. Brenner, J. Brown, and D. Canter (eds.), *The Research Interview: Uses and Approaches.* London: Academic Press, 1985.

Campbell, D. T. "Reforms as Experiments." *American Psychologist,* 1969, *24,* 409-428.

Canter, D., Brown, J., and Groat, L. "A Multiple Sorting Procedure for Studying Conceptual Systems." In M. Brenner, J. Brown, and D. Canter (eds.), *The Research Interview: Uses and Approaches.* London: Academic Press, 1985.

Chen, H.-T., and Rossi, P. H. "The Multi-Goal, Theory-Driven Approach to Evaluation: A Model Linking Basic and Applied Social Science." In H. E. Freeman and M. A. Solomon (eds.), *Evaluation Studies Review Annual.* Vol. 6. Beverly Hills, Calif.: Sage, 1981.

Chen, H.-T., and Rossi, P. H. "Evaluating with Sense: The Theory-Driven Approach." *Evaluation Review,* 1983, *7,* 283-302.

Cook, T. D., and Campbell, D. T. *Quasi-Experimentation Design: Design and Analysis Issues for Field Settings.* Skokie, Ill.: Rand McNally, 1979.

Cook, T. D., Leviton, L. C., and Shadish, W. R., Jr. "Program Evaluation." In G. Lindzey and E. Aronson (eds.), *Handbook of Social Psychology.* (3rd ed.) New York: Random House, 1985.

Cook, T. D., and Shadish, W. R., Jr. "Program Evaluation: The Worldly Science." *Annual Review of Psychology,* 1986, *37,* 193-232.

Cronbach, L. J. *Designing Evaluations of Education and Social Programs.* San Francisco: Jossey-Bass, 1982.

Edwards, J., Hotch, D., and Bickman, L. "Measuring Children's Health-Related Attitudes and Knowledge." In L. Bickman (ed.), *Applied Social Psychology Annual.* Vol. 3. Beverly Hills, Calif.: Sage, 1982.

Janis, I. L., and Mann, L. *Decision Making: A Psychological Analysis on Conflict, Choice, and Commitment.* New York: Free Press, 1977.

Lipsey, M. W., Crosse, S., Dunkle, J., Pollard, J., and Stobart, G. "Evaluation: The State of the Art and the Sorry State of Science." In D. S. Cordray (ed.), *Utilizing Prior Research in Evaluation Planning.* New Directions for Program Evaluation, no. 27. San Francisco: Jossey-Bass, 1985.

Lord, C. G., Ross, and Lepper, M. R. "Biased Assimilation and Attitude Polarization: The Effects of Prior Theories on Subsequently Considered Evidence." *Journal of Personality and Social Psychology,* 1979, *37,* 2098-2109.

Rog, D., and Bickman, L. "The Feedback Research Approach to Evaluation: A

Method to Increase Evaluation Utility." *Evaluation and Program Planning*, 1984, 7, 169–175.

Rutman, L. *Planning Useful Evaluations: Evaluability Assessment*. Beverly Hills, Calif.: Sage, 1980.

Scheirer, M. A. *Program Implementation: The Organizational Context*. Beverly Hills, Calif.: Sage, 1981.

Scriven, M. *The Logic of Evaluation*. Inverness, Calif.: Edgepress, 1980.

Scriven, M. "Evaluation Ideologies." In G. F. Madavs, M. Scriven, and D. L. Stuffelbeam (eds.), *Evaluation Models: Viewpoints on Educational and Human Services Evaluation*. Boston, Mass.: Klower-Nijhoff, 1983.

Shaklee, H., and Fischoff, B. "Strategies of Information Search and Causal Analysis." *Memory and Cognition*, 1982, *10*, 520–530.

Stake, R. E. "The Case Study Method in Social Inquiry." *Educational Research*, 1978, 7, 5–8.

Suchman, E. A. *Evaluative Research: Principles and Practice in Public Service and Social Action Programs*. New York: Russell Sage Foundation, 1967.

Weick, K. E., and Bougon, M. G. "Organization as Cognitive Maps." In H. P. Simms, Jr., and D. A. Gioia (eds.), *Social Cognition in Organizations*. San Francisco: Jossey-Bass, 1986.

Weiss, C. H. *Evaluation Research: Methods for Assessing Program Effectiveness*. Inglewood Cliffs, N. J.: Prentice-Hall, 1972.

Wholey, J. S. "Evaluability Assessment." In L. Rutman (ed.), *Evaluative Research Methods: A Basic Guide*. Beverly Hills, Calif.: Sage, 1977.

Wholey, J. S. *Evaluation: Promise and Performance*. Washington, D.C.: Urban Institute, 1979.

*Leonard Bickman is professor of psychology at Peabody College, Vanderbilt University. He is director of the Program Evaluation Laboratory at Peabody and director of the Center for Mental Health Policy at the Vanderbilt Institute for Public Policy Studies.*

*Program philosophy includes theories and values. An
evaluation is made more coherent by measuring the
philosophy and testing its implementation and effectiveness.*

# Measuring and Testing Program Philosophy

*Kendon J. Conrad, Todd Q. Miller*

This chapter addresses two closely related problems in program evaluation.
The first is how to specify in measurable terms the consensus of theories
and values (the philosophy) that guides the program. The second is how to
construct a theoretical framework that specifies how these measurements
are to be used in evaluating programs (that is, testing the implementation
and effectiveness of the philosophy). This chapter briefly reviews the history
of the problems, states the underlying assumptions, proposes a framework
for testing program philosophy, and provides several illustrations of how
to measure program philosophy. It also suggests how to use these measures
in verifying appropriate implementation and interpreting outcomes.

## A Brief History

In the late 1950s, 1960s, and throughout the 1970s there was a
general recognition by evaluation theorists that full description of programs was essential (for example, Medley and Mitzel, 1958; Stake, 1967;

The authors are grateful to Geneva Haertel, Maurice Eash, William
Revelle, Leonard Bickman, and Joseph Wholey for their thoughtful comments on
earlier drafts of this chapter and to Cynthia Walters for manuscript assistance.

L. Bickman (ed.). *Using Program Theory in Evaluation.*
New Directions for Program Evaluation, no. 33. San Francisco: Jossey-Bass, Spring 1987.

see McGrath, 1984, for a review). However, the sudden surge of social programs, the need for timely evaluation of these programs, and the strong conviction that the programs would work contributed to a decline in research including process measures (a time-consuming activity with few proponents and fewer practitioners) and to the encouragement of studies designed to test input-output links directly (Campbell and Stanley, 1963; Chen and Rossi, 1983; Worthen and Sanders, 1973).

*The Follow Through Evaluation.* One evaluation that attempted to be an exception to this trend was the evaluation of the Follow Through Program (Haney, 1977; McDaniels, 1975). Follow Through was a compensatory education program for school-aged, low-income children and was designed to continue the advantages provided to preschoolers by the Head Start Program (Westinghouse . . . , 1969). The Follow Through evaluation was a planned variation quasiexperiment that attempted to assess the differential impact of a variety of educational philosophies and strategies. Two of the Follow Through evaluation's principal research questions were: Do the various educational strategies used in Follow Through have different effects, and is there a relationship between the extent of a given treatment's implementation and its impact?

In order to answer these questions it was necessary that two situations occur. First, philosophical differences in curriculum should be translated into distinctive classroom atmospheres. Second, the fidelity of a particular site to its planned curriculum philosophy would have to be assessed. As McDaniels (1975) notes, "To the extent that such questions are not clearly answered (or are unanswerable), the planned variation design is of dubious methodological value" (p. 8).

Unfortunately the Follow Through evaluation lacked the reliable and valid measures of fidelity to its curriculum philosophy necessary for the interpretation of the results. How would these implementation measures have been useful? They would have provided empirical evidence that the Follow Through models were actually different from each other as well as different from customary programs. They would have identified sites that were successful at implementing the intended curriculum philosophy. They would have provided evidence of "seepage," or diffusion, of the experimental treatments into the comparison groups. They would have enabled the assessment of fidelity and level of implementation over time, across changing administrations, staffs, children, and so on. In brief, a methodology for measuring and testing the program philosophies of the Follow Through models would have made the outcomes more readily interpretable.

*Recent Developments.* Recently, there has been a renewal of interest in the assessment of program characteristics (Scheirer and Rezmovic, 1983) because experimental and quasiexperimental input-output evaluations without measures of philosophy, structure, and process have several weaknesses. Experimental evaluations focusing on outcomes are often impractical, have limited generalizability, and typically convey limited or no information about why the program does or does not work. Quasiexperimental studies pose additional threats to causal inference about program effectiveness (Cook and Campbell, 1979). As a result of the difficulties with evaluations focusing on outcomes, some evaluators are becoming less interested in the simple question of whether the program works and are becoming more interested in discovering how and why a program works by examining the relationships among philosophy, implementation, and outcome (Chen and Rossi, 1983). Therefore, it has become apparent to these evaluators that more information about program philosophies and their implementation is needed in order to make valid causal attributions about programs, projects, and elements (Quay, 1979). Unfortunately, there are few available measures of program philosophies and their implementation, and construction of such measures is no easy task (Rezmovic, 1984), often requiring complex methodological and theoretical considerations (Bickman, 1985; Cook, Leviton, and Shadish, 1985).

Evaluations of program implementation usually attempt to measure the degree of success in delivering program elements (Cook, Leviton, and Shadish, 1985; Wholey, 1979) and will often measure the abilities of staff and physical resources as well as staff cohesiveness, but it is unusual for a study to include measures of the philosophy of the program or the group consensus of theories and values. There is, in fact, a growing awareness that our studies of program implementation require such measures (Lemke and Moos, 1986). Assessing the appropriateness of implementation implies the setting of standards (values) and the determination of quality. It appears that quality cannot be determined using easily measured structure and process criteria alone. Rather, the setting of quality standards depends on the values and goals imbedded in the program philosophy. Moos (1980), for example, states that the institutional structure of residential settings for the elderly "commonly arises out of a general philosophy about residents which also manifests itself in other ways" (p. 84).

As another example, the federal government currently uses survey procedures for assessing nursing homes for compliance with minimum conditions of participation for either the Medicare or Medicaid program. The survey focuses on structural requirements such as written policies and procedures, staff qualifications and functions, the presence of specific agreements and contracts, and the physical plant. The assumption underlying these procedures is that, if the structural requirements are met, the desired goal (that is, high-quality care or appropriate implementation of the program philosophy) will be attained. However, a Denver court ruling in 1984 in the *Smith* v. *Heckler* lawsuit held that measuring structural factors could not be equated with measuring quality of care. Consequently, new procedures are being devised that attempt to address directly the appropriate delivery of the major elements of the program philosophy.

Linn, Gurel, and Linn (1977) provide an example of the need to measure program philosophy that arises out of the frustration of researchers in measuring the major elements of complex social programs. These investigators attempted to measure the structural and process indicators (such as medical records, available services, general policies, meals, accreditation, staffing, and physical facilities) of nursing homes that accounted for improved patient outcomes, but they expressed the belief that philosophical and attitudinal factors were more likely to be responsible for outcomes. Additionally, Linn states, "Certainly, there are minimum standards below which homes cannot fall without affecting quality, but it may be that once these standards are met that it is other factors, such as the kind of atmosphere of the home or personalities of the staff, that influence patient outcome. Unfortunately, these are qualities not so easily measured" (Linn, Gurel, and Linn, 1977, p. 342).

**Definitions and Assumptions**

Program philosophy is that system of theories and values that defines and guides the structure, population, process, and outcomes of the program. This definition assumes that the philosophy comes before the physical and behavioral manifestations of the program, a deductive perspective. This perspective enables experimental methods; that is, the statement of hypotheses and their subsequent testing. Moreover, it provides a framework for comparison across different evaluations (Chen and Rossi, 1983).

Our assumption is that the program philosophy determines the ways in which programs attempt to meet their clients' needs. This perspective holds that the need arises and existing theories and values are activated to meet the need. Therefore, the theories and values exist prior to the needs, but the needs activate their use. Given this basic temporal and logical sequence, it is also true that the philosophy develops and changes along with the structure, process, population, and outcome of the program (Cooley and Lohnes, 1974; Moos, 1980). The program philosophy is stable but not static.

The foundation for our assumptions about the nature and importance of measuring program philosophy lies in sociological theory, curriculum theory, and studies of group interaction. The assumption is supported by a large body of theory and research that holds that every group needs a set of values and that a pattern of activity must be maintained in line with these values if the group is to have integrity (Brickman and others, 1982; Hare, 1983; McGrath and Kravitz, 1982; Parsons, 1960; Tuckman, 1965; Tyler, 1950). As expressed by Parsons (1960), sociological theory holds that "the main point of reference for analyzing the structure of any social system is its value pattern. This defines the basic orientation of the system (in the present case, the organization) to the situation in which it operates; hence it guides the activities of participant individuals" (p. 20). Hare calls this set of values "latent pattern maintenance," Tuckman calls it "forming," and McGrath calls it "values and goals." We prefer the term *philosophy* because it means basically the same thing; is a common parlance often used in program guides, curriculum guides, and so forth; and is general enough to include all of the preceding terms.

*Theories and Values.* Programs are not simply manifestations of theories of behavioral or social change. In fact they are value laden (Brickman and others, 1982; Worthen and Sanders, 1973) and guided by traditions of common practice; ethical, religious, and political beliefs; and vague ideas about how to affect complex social processes. Implicit in the statement that program philosophy is composed of theories and values is that program philosophy includes statements about goals. Theories tell how to accomplish goals. Values determine the goals to be accomplished and the theories to be employed in accomplishing them. In addition, the performance criteria used in monitoring program implementation are invariably value laden (Ezrahi, 1978) and depend on a priori judgments. "Evaluators need to explicate the values implicit in each criterion and standard of comparison they consider" (Cook, Leviton, and Shadish, 1985).

In program evaluation a particular philosophy is a theory insofar as it is a selected set of statements about causes and their effects (goals) that stands concurrently in agreement with and in opposition to other statements. The range of these statements composes the body of theory, that is, the existing repertoire of putative causes and effects in a field of endeavor. The existence of a program philosophy implies the choice (valuing) of a particular set of statements, a theory. Therefore, a program philosophy includes a theory or theories but goes beyond theory insofar as it combines value statements with statements about causes and effects. For a particular project, this combination results in statements designed to guide behavior.

Values are different from theories in that they contain moral, personal, and emotion-laden qualities. While theories usually determine the structure, values determine the cohesiveness and role patterns of the organization. It is important to state values as well as theories because, while theories state how to achieve objectives, values provide the emotion-arousal qualities of motivation. A congruence between values and theories is a prerequisite to successful program implementation (Tuckman, 1965). Since values are the product of one's professional training and culture (Rokeach, 1968), they are probably more stable than program theories and therefore are more likely to have a long-lasting and pervasive effect on the organization.

*Programs, Projects, and Elements.* This chapter adopts the definitions used by Cook, Leviton, and Shadish (1985) when referring to programs, projects, and elements. In brief, programs serve as blueprints, guiding and coordinating local projects: for example, the Head Start Program, the Community Mental Health Center Program, the Chicago Child Parent Center Program. At the program level the philosophy or intentions of the program should be clearly stated to serve as a guide for the projects or individual sites. Projects are local centers that coordinate the activities intended by the program for which program funds are received, such as the North Memphis Community Mental Health Center or the Hansberry Child Parent Center. The projects provide the means or structure needed for carrying out the intentions of the program. In most evaluations the assumption is made that the staff philosophy at the project level conforms to the program philosophy. This is by no means a safe assumption (Cook, Leviton, and Shadish, 1985), and this is one reason why it is necessary to measure program philosophy at both levels. Elements are components within a project or program that the evaluator's critical analysis of the program philosophy suggests may be necessary for appropriate implementation or useful for bringing about desired effects. Examples of elements include lunches cooked on school premises as opposed to lunches prepared centrally and served as cold snacks or parent involvement in classroom activities.

## Need to Measure Program Philosophy

Hare (1983), in one of the most recent papers on this topic, states that obtaining consensus on underlying values and goals (intentions) is the first and most important problem of groups (see Figure 1). This consensus guides the solution to the subsequent problems of developing the abilities and resources to attain goals (means or structure) and developing norms to guide goal behavior and cohesiveness to support norms (means or structure). Once resources are obtained and norms and cohesiveness are developed, the group is able to solve the fourth fundamental problem of groups, effective group task performance (action or process).

In the context of program evaluation, values and goals may be considered the program philosophy or the consensus of theories and values at the central administrative level that precedes, guides, and controls the implementation of the program at the individual sites or projects. Resources is defined similarly in evaluation, but norms and cohesiveness are more clearly understood as the integration of or agreement with the program philosophy by the people responsible for its implementation at the project level (that is, project philosophy). In other words, if the program is to be implemented as intended, it is important that the project staff integrate or agree with the basic theories and values composing the program philosophy. Group task performance may be understood more specifically as the delivery of the intended program elements.

## Figure 1. Hare's Four Problems of Group Interaction

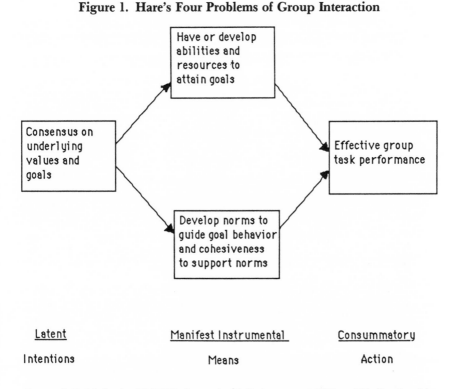

*Source:* J. E. McGrath, *GROUPS: Interaction & Performance,* © 1984, p. 160. Reprinted by permission of Prentice-Hall, Inc., Englewood Cliffs, New Jersey.

The general assumptions (input-process-output) of the causal model in Figure 1 have been supported by previous small group research (for a review, see Hackman and Morris, 1975). However, in spite of the fact that theorists recognize the importance of program philosophy, little has been done to define the concept through systematic study or to measure its implementation. When the capability of measuring the general philosophical consensus or the various pockets of consensus has been developed, it is possible to specify more clearly the structure and process components that are congruent with that consensus.

### A Program Development Model

To understand the use of program philosophy measures in program evaluation, it is necessary to explicate a model of how programs are developed, implemented, and evaluated. In Figure 2, panels 1 and 2 depict such a model. We will describe the steps in this model in the following section.

## Figure 2. A Philosophy-Testing Evaluation

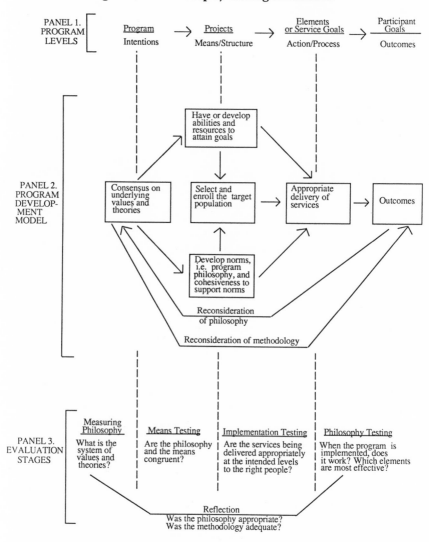

*The Program Level: Intentions.* The program is conceived when a consensus of theories and values develops that clarifies a need for and the means to the accomplishment of a goal. When the consensus is general and powerful enough, funding is appropriate to purchase the resources necessary for the accomplishment of the goal.

*The Project Level: Means/Structure.* The funding is administered at the program level to projects that should conform, within clear boundaries, to the philosophical, structural, and process norms of the program. The funding enables the provision of the abilities and resources needed to attain goals. Under the leadership of dedicated practitioners, local projects develop the group norms and cohesiveness necessary for the accomplishment of the task. In our terminology, this means that people are hired who conform to the program philosophy and/or they are educated about the intentions of the program. Using program guidelines regarding the target population, clients are selected and enrolled.

*Elements or Service Goals: Action/Process.* The implementation of resources and group norms and cohesiveness as well as the enrollment of the target population enable the appropriate delivery of services. Service delivery is the interaction of resources and group norms and cohesiveness with the target population. Measuring service delivery may simply mean ascertaining that the program components and the program recipients come into contact with each other (exposure). A count of these encounters would be a basic and necessary, but often relatively uninformative, measure of service delivery. A more informative approach would be to measure the amount of contact in order to gauge how much of the program the recipients received (the dosage). Amount of contact can be measured by such things as the amount of time spent in an activity, or the amount of materials (food, books, medicine) consumed.

In evaluating social programs it is informative to measure the type of contact made. As used here, implementation measures include instruments or indicators that measure types of contact specified as necessary to obtain the intended outcomes. Therefore, this chapter deals not only with the simple implementation question "Did the encounter between program components and participants take place?" but also with the questions "What was the nature of the program? Were the program components implemented at the intended levels? How did the experimental program as delivered differ from the customary treatment?" Implied in the last question is the necessity of measuring both the experimental program and the customary treatment.

*Participant Goals: Outcomes.* Service delivery results in participant outcomes. The outcomes may cause a reconsideration or confirmation of the philosophy, but depending on how controversial they are, they will also bring the evaluation methodology under closer scrutiny and more severe criticism.

The following passage states well the point that success at each of these levels is essential and that the levels are interdependent: "Considered as a whole, a program can be conceived as a system in which each element is dependent on the other. Unless money is supplied, no facilities can be built, no new jobs can flow from them, and no . . . personnel can be hired to fill them. A breakdown at one stage must be repaired, therefore, before it is possible to move on to the next. The stages are related, however, from back to front as well as from front to back. Failure to agree on procedures for hiring . . . may lead the government to withhold funds, thus halting the construction. Program implementation thus becomes a seamless web" (Pressman and Wildavsky, 1973). One component of the evaluator's job is to test for the presence of seams, and it is important to be aware that the common thread running through all components is the program philosophy.

## Evaluation Stages

In a philosophy-testing evaluation the evaluator needs the ability to measure the philosophy, project resources and abilities, group norms and cohesiveness, the target population, and the elements necessary for the accomplishment of the goals. Then it is the evaluator's job to test projects in regard to their conformity/fidelity to the intentions of the program. The following problems are of concern in this chapter: (1) In actual practice the program philosophy may not be clearly and accurately stated at the program level; (2) even if it is clearly and accurately stated at the program level, empirical methods for measuring conformity at the project level are lacking; (3) whether it is or is not clearly stated, very different, idiosyncratic, or even opposing models may spring up at the project level, and the evaluator needs methods for distinguishing among the models in order to evaluate them.

In a philosophy-testing evaluation (Figure 2, panel 3) the evaluator must do five things: (1) measuring philosophy, or delineating the characteristics of the program's system(s) of theories and values and developing methods for measuring their existence; (2) means testing, or checking to see that the projects agree with and have integrated the program philosophy and conform in terms of resources, cohesiveness, and target population of the program; (3) implementation testing, or checking to see that services are actually being delivered appropriately at the intended levels to the right people; (4) philosophy testing, or checking to see that when the program is implemented it achieves the intended goals; and (5) reflection, or reconsidering the appropriateness of the philosophy given the outcomes as well as reconsidering the appropriateness of the evaluation methodology. Owing to the limited scope of this chapter, we will simply note that in experimental and quasiexperimental evaluations these stages apply not only to the experimental group but also to the control group. Therefore, it is necessary to measure in all stages of the evaluation how or that the experimental program is different from the customary condition or treatment.

*Measuring Philosophy.* In this stage the evaluator first asks if a consensus of theories and values really exists. If so, of what does this consensus consist? The answers to these questions can be obtained from the program guide; a review of the literature; discussions with and surveys of stakeholders; observations of and participation in pilot projects; discussions with program decision makers and other stakeholders to clarify the statements of the philosophy; and surveys of project administration, staff, and clients.

*Means Testing.* When the statements and consensus are clarified, it is necessary to measure the congruence between the philosophy and the means specified for its actualization. Do the projects have adequate space and equipment? Are they staffed with people who have the appropriate philosophy, skills, and abilities? Have the staff members integrated the program philosophy? Do they agree with the goals of the program and on how the goals should be accomplished? Are they selecting and enrolling clients with appropriate characteristics? For example, Roberts-Gray (1985) treats these issues in discussing strategies to facilitate changes in user characteristics so that features of the innovative program can be accommodated: "These changes establish the fit that is needed between innovation and user so that the desired degree of implementation will be realized" (p. 262). In other words, the means testing stage tests the congruence of the project philosophy with the program philosophy.

*Implementation Testing.* Given the existence of the means required for the implementation of the program, it should follow that the program will be implemented, but it does not necessarily follow that the program will be implemented appropriately at the intended levels to all of the targeted clients. Therefore, it is necessary to measure the elements of service delivery. This means determining that the resources are being used appropriately at the intended levels, that the staff members' behavior is congruent with their theories and values, and that the people who are enrolled are receiving services congruent with their needs.

*Philosophy Testing.* The appropriate implementation of the philosophy should result in the delivery of services. Therefore, a test of the effectiveness of the services in causing the intended outcomes is a test of the philosophy. In this context, those relationships should be stated a priori and tested by examining relationships among measures of services and measures of outcomes. Appropriate statistical techniques depend on the nature of the particular problem but usually will include regression analysis and structural equation modeling owing to their usefulness in examining complex causal relationships (Judd and Kenny, 1981). We again note that in testing the effectiveness of a new program relative to customary treatment, a program causal model should be constructed for the customary treatment as well, and its elements should also be measured (for example, see Conrad, 1983).

*Reflection.* When the evaluation outcomes are reported, stakeholders will reflect on two major concerns: the appropriateness of the philosophy and the adequacy of the methodology. For example, the evaluation of the Head Start Program found, generally, that the program had no effect in improving preschoolers' readiness for school (Westinghouse . . . , 1969). In fact, there were erroneous indications that the program was harmful (for a discussion, see Campbell and Erlebacher, 1970). As a result of these findings, there was a general questioning of the strongly held belief that preschool compensatory education would be clearly beneficial. The high aspirations and expectations of the Head Start philosophy had to be modified to more realistic levels. Based on these findings and the aura of doubt they created, the Nixon administration drastically cut the Head Start budget. However, questioning of the philosophy resulted in a counter wave of reflection on the adequacy of the evaluation methodology. Subsequently, more rigorous evaluations have demonstrated successful outcomes for programs with adequate implementation (Conrad and Eash, 1983).

The foregoing program development model breaks down at its inception if there is not a clear, detailed specification of the program's philosophy, structure, population, process, and outcomes. In our first example we will discuss methods of delineating the program philosophy, since this is the first and most neglected phase in the model.

## When Philosophical Definition Is Needed

To assess appropriate implementation of the program philosophy, it is necessary that there be a clear specification of the philosophy. In the early development of many programs, there is a vague and general consensus that there is a need for a program but no clear, detailed specification of the characteristics of the program. Funding is provided under a general rubric to local projects, which develop a reasonable philosophy in answer to the need. When this situation exists there is a clear need for philosophical definition if we are to assess implementation and evaluate the program. The following example will illustrate one procedure for defining and measuring the program philosophy.

*Programs for Adolescents with Behavioral Disorders.* In 1981 the first author became involved in an evaluation of a project serving adolescents with behavioral disorders. In the course of designing this evaluation, it became clear that there were many different kinds of projects within this general category. The need to define and categorize these different classes of projects led to the following study, which will serve as an example of the case in which philosophical definition is needed.

In 1975 Public Law 94-142, the Education for All Handicapped Children Act, mandated that all children with handicaps be provided an appropriate free education in the least restrictive environment. Previous to PL 94-142, many schools commonly failed to provide services for handicapped children, especially those with behavioral disorders. Since 1975, then, alternative school programs for adolescents with severe behavioral disorders have or should have sprung up throughout the country in response to the mandate of PL 94-142.

*A Lack of Consensus.* In regard to the existence of a clear philosophical or theoretical consensus on the functioning of behavioral disorders (BD) programs, Sabatino and Mauser (1978) report that the current literature was devoid "of any organized means of examining the high school curriculum to account for chronic disruptive youth" (p. 40). To further support this conclusion, Brown and Palmer (1977) in their review of Bureau of Educationally Handicapped funded personnel preparation programs in emotional disturbance, state that "programs focusing on the skills and competencies necessary for setting up quality educational programs at the secondary level simply do not exist in most areas of the country" (p. 173).

Clearly, the effectiveness of PL 94-142 in creating better programs and treatment for BD adolescents was unknown. Additionally, it was not clear what types of school BD programs existed. Therefore, it was the objective of this study to develop the ability to classify projects into distinguishable philosophical models. This ability would enable evaluators to clarify what it was they were evaluating before attempting to draw inferences about its effectiveness.

*Whom to Ask.* Given the constraint of a limited budget, it was decided that the most cost-effective and appropriate strategy for gathering data about BD program models would be to ask questions of the on-site project directors. The on-site directors, it was thought, would be the best single source of information because they were responsible for the overall direction of the daily activities of the projects. Since, in general, the projects would be relatively small (averaging about forty students), the project directors would have intimate knowledge of most activities, and they would be very influential in shaping the philosophical bent of the project (for a discussion of the role of professional judgment in evaluation, see Stake, 1967). We recognized that to measure philosophical consensus at the project level, it would be necessary to survey administrators, staff, and clients. However, we were interested in definition and categorization at the program level; therefore, a good sample of projects to obtain representation of philosophical models was more appropriate and efficient.

*How to Ask: Developing a Conceptual Map.* Once we decided whom to ask, we needed to decide how to ask them. Open-ended questions would be too unstructured and therefore difficult to interpret. We needed questions that would cover the major currents of thought on the treatment of BD adolescents. We turned to the literature and found a general model depicting the major theories in emotional disturbance (Apter, 1982; Morse, Smith, and Acker, 1978) as represented in Figure 3. This conceptual map of theories of treatment served as a guideline in the development of items, but it was not enough to educate us about the actual hands-on elements of the programs. As a result, we made repeated site visits to two projects with apparently opposing treatment philosophies, one behavioristic and the other psychodynamic. Site visits included direct observation, conversations with administrators, staff, and students, and participation in the activities. In the case of the behavioristic project, the first author participated in the staff training activities. We felt this gave us a good understanding and appreciation of the issues. Our conversations gave us statements useful for constructing items. Additionally, leaders in the field were consulted, and thereby the validity of the conceptual map was confirmed and more items were derived. The items were reviewed by staff and experts, with this process resulting in a forty-one-item questionnaire. These items were categorized a priori into seven scales (Table 1), which were, in general, representative of the domains on the conceptual map depicted in Figure 3.

*How to Ask: Administering the Questionnaire.* The questionnaire was distributed as part of a survey of 182 public and 56 private school BD programs in Illinois. The respondents represented every area of Illinois, including large and small urban, suburban, and rural areas. Seventy percent of the respondents classified themselves as administrators and the rest were teachers. This sampling frame was considered representative of the population of on-site program directors and teachers of high school BD programs having at least one self-contained classroom. Of the 238 programs in the final sampling frame, 180 (76 percent) usable questionnaires were returned. One hundred and forty public programs responded (78 percent), and 40 private programs responded (69 percent). Response rates were similar for public, private, urban, and rural programs.

*Analyzing the Data.* Our first major question concerned whether the responses of the directors would cluster into the a priori scales we had delineated. To analyze the Likert scale items, a seven-stage cluster analysis was performed in which cluster solutions were obtained for seven scales, then six, and so on. Goodness-of-fit estimates were obtained that demonstrated that the three-scale solution was best (Revelle, 1979).

The results of the cluster analysis are depicted in Table 2. Thirty-one of the forty-one items formed three scales. The remaining items were dropped from the analysis because of their weak loadings on these scales. Based on the content of their items, the scales were given the following names: expectation of personal responsibility, program control of student behavior, and psychodynamic versus behavioristic philosophy. The Cronbach's alphas, cluster loadings, and sample items are shown in the tables.

## Figure 3. A Conceptual Map of Major Theories
## in Emotional Disturbance

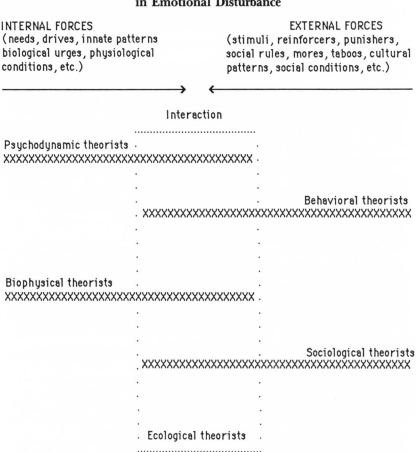

INTERNAL FORCES
(needs, drives, innate patterns
biological urges, physiological
conditions, etc.)

EXTERNAL FORCES
(stimuli, reinforcers, punishers,
social rules, mores, taboos, cultural
patterns, social conditions, etc.)

Interaction

Psychodynamic theorists

Behavioral theorists

Biophysical theorists

Sociological theorists

Ecological theorists

*Source:* S. J. Apter, *Troubled Children/Troubled Systems,* © 1982, p. 17. Reprinted by permission of Permagon Press, Elmsford, New York.

An alpha of 0.7 is regarded as fair reliability with 0.9 being excellent, and 0.5 being poor. The psychodynamic versus behavioristic philosophy scale was composed in large part of psychodynamic items. The administrative control scale was predominantly made up of administration-centered and student-centered items. The expectation of personal responsibility scale had the three existential items, with the highest loadings for most others being administration-centered and behavior modification items.

We had found that four of our a priori scales reduced to two cluster analysis scales simply because they were opposite viewpoints on the same dimension, that is, administration-centered versus student-centered and psychodynamic versus behavioristic. The third scale to explain substantial

## Table 1. A Priori Classification of BD Item Descriptors

Psychodynamic Items:
1. The program emphasizes changing the inappropriate behaviors of students through discussing them.
5. Changing problem behaviors is a process which takes years to accomplish.
12. Treatment for behavior problems should provide insight into past conflicts.
32. There is a great emphasis placed on learning about students' feelings.
37. Changing a child's behavior is less important than dealing with the underlying conflicts which cause the behavior.
39. The arts, including music and dance, are important components of the therapy program.

Behavior Modification Items:
8. Teachers give points or tokens for appropriate behavior.
9. Teachers are expected to be models of appropriate behavior.
14. All problem behaviors are learned and can be unlearned.
15. Teachers take away privileges of students for inappropriate behaviors.
27. This program focuses on changing problem behaviors before dealing with internal psychological processes.
29. This program employs locked isolation rooms.
34. Staff members will sometimes ignore students in order to manipulate their behavior.

Student-Centered Items:
2. If students become violent or uncontrollable, they are sent home.
3. Students have freedom in choosing their class schedules.
6. Students may leave school any time they want without obtaining permission.
7. This program encourages student control of the school environment.
17. Students get to school any way they choose.
19. There is a smoking area for students in the school building.
21. Students are free to determine their own daily routine.
23. Students are not forced to go to classes.
30. Students are expected to take leadership here.
31. If students behave inappropriately, they can be suspended from school.

Administration-Centered Items:
10. Students stick closely to a routine which is defined by the administration.
16. Staff rarely give in to pressure from students.
18. Students are sometimes kept after school as a consequence of inappropriate behavior.
22. Students are not allowed to move about the classroom without asking permission.
25. Staff are trained in methods of physical restraint.
26. Students need permission to go to the washroom.
28. This program has a high degree of control over student behaviors.
33. Staff must win all power struggles with students.
36. Teachers sometimes control students by restraining them.

Existential Items:
4. Behavior problems are principally a result of a lack of responsibility for one's behavior.
11. This program demands that students assume personal responsibility for their behavior.
24. The major responsibility for the child's behavior resides with the child.

Ecological Items:
13. This program emphasizes changing the child's environment outside of school.
20. This program primarily relies on peer pressure to control student behavior.
38. Behavior disorders are primarily caused by a bad fit between the particular child and the environment.

Biophysical Items:
35. Behavior disorders are primarily the result of physiological factors.
40. Drugs are administered as part of the school program.

## Table 2. Scales, Alphas,[a] and Sample Items[b]
## of the BD Program Processes Scale

| | |
|---|---|
| Scale name: | Expectation of Personal Responsibility (Alpha=.68, n of items=7) |
| Sample items: (loading) | 1. This program demands that students assume personal responsibility for their behavior. (.736) |
| | 2. The major responsibility for the child's behavior resides with the child. (.578) |
| | 3. Behavior problems are principally a result of a lack of responsibility for one's behavior. (.567) |
| | 4. Staff rarely give in to pressure from students. (.475) |
| | 5. Students are expected to take leadership here. (.449) |
| Scale name: | Program Control of Student Behavior (alpha=.73, n of items=10) |
| Sample Items: (loading) | 1. Staff are trained in methods of physical restraint. (.713) |
| | 2. This program employs locked isolation rooms. (.578) |
| | 3. If students behave inappropriately, they can be suspended from school. (-.539) |
| | 4. Teachers sometimes control students by restraining them. (.534) |
| | 5. If students become violent or uncontrollable, they are sent home. (-.517) |
| Scale name: | Psychodynamic vs. Behavioristic Orientation (alpha=.66, n of items =10) |
| Sample items: (loading) | 1. There is a great emphasis placed on learning about students' feelings. (.598) |
| | 2. Treatment for behavior problems should provide insight into past conflicts. (.511) |
| | 3. This program focuses on changing problem behaviors before dealing with internal psychological processes. (-.482) |
| | 4. The arts, including music and dance, are important components of the therapy program. (.454) |
| | 5. This program emphasizes changing the child's enviornment outside of school. (.421) |

[a] Alpha is Cronbach's estimate of internal consistency.

[b] A negative loading indicates that the item was reversed or, in other words, is the oposite of the positive items.

variance in the responses of the directors was the expectation of personal responsibility scale composed mainly of the existentialism items. The ecological and biophysical items did not form separate scales. From these data we concluded that we had derived three scales that were useful in describing the philosophical approaches of school programs for BD adolescents. The scales had only fair (around 0.7) reliability, but this could be improved in subsequent studies.

The correlations of the scales with each other and with the other elements that were measured provided an estimate of the construct validity of the scales. In other words, the correlations indicated whether the scales were really measuring what they seemed to be measuring. For example, program control should have been and was positively correlated with elements such as use of time-out rooms, being a residential facility, higher attendance, being or having a self-contained BD classroom, and administrator's perception of severity of the student population. Psychodynamic versus behavioristic philosophy should have been positively correlated with the presence of and participation in counseling programs. This was not consistently the case. It makes good sense that expectation of personal responsibility should be correlated with career training, work-study, and job placement, and this was the case. Regarding the correlations of the scales with each other, it was expected that psychodynamic versus behavioristic should be negatively correlated with the control and expectation scales, and this was the case.

*Conclusions.* An instrument measuring the philosophy of school programs for adolescents with behavioral disorders was analyzed and found to have fair reliability. One scale, program control of student behavior, appeared to have excellent construct validity. The data did not strongly support the construct validity of the psychodynamic versus behavioristic philosophy scale, but it was not clear if this was due to a lack of validity in the scale or the fact that the philosophical statements which people espoused were simply not in accord with their behavior as measured in the survey. The cluster analysis revealed a third scale named expectation of personal responsibility, which was significantly correlated with items indicating that programs included career training or job placement.

Generally, the evidence supports the usefulness of the scales in measuring the philosophy of BD programs. Therefore, this study developed the capability of measuring program philosophy. These measures are now available for use in classifying BD projects as part of an evaluation of the effectiveness of different models. In another example, Lemke and Moos (1980) have constructed and used such instruments in composing program profiles that may be used to categorize classes of programs.

### When Program Philosophy Has Been Defined

To illustrate some of the instrument development tasks and procedures involved in means testing and implementation testing (see Figure 2) when the program philosophy is clearly stated, we will describe an evaluation that is currently being developed by the Health Services Research and Development Service of the Veterans Administration (VA). Although the VA evaluation is in the design stage, we believe that its instrumentation is worth discussing because of its coverage of the important components of a philosophy testing evaluation.

*Context.* The VA is bracing itself for a dramatic increase in demand for care due to the increased needs of the large group of aging veterans who served in World War II and the Korean War. One component of a seven-part strategy for improving services to elderly veterans is the development of Adult Day Health Care (ADHC) programs at VA facilities. The

VA model of ADHC is designed to meet the needs of patients at high risk for nursing home placement and to substitute for such placements.

*Clarifying Intentions.* To test a philosophy it is necessary to have a clear statement of that philosophy. It is the existence of this clear statement and consensus at the program level that enables the subsequent steps in a philosophy testing evaluation. The ADHC program in the VA had this clear statement and consensus. As specified in the program guidelines, ADHC is a "therapeutically oriented ambulatory day program which provides health, maintenance, and rehabilitative services to frail individuals in a congregate setting during daytime hours" (Veterans Administration, 1984, p. 8). The program guidelines provided very detailed specifications of the elements required of ADHC programs in the VA, including provision for medical evaluation, medication, prescriptions, treatment, personal care, nutrition, transportation, social activities, and follow-up. This model of ADHC is clearly medical (as opposed to social) in its philosophical orientation.

In a subcontract to the overall evaluation, the first author was asked to develop measures of the structures and processes of ADHC that would be useful in verifying the appropriate implementation of the program and in providing information about the causal processes of ADHC. The resulting project developed and field tested the Adult Day Care Assessment Procedure (ADCAP), a set of five instruments designed to characterize the program philosophy, the physical and social environments, and the treatment processes of the ADHC program in the VA (Conrad, Rothman, and Miller, 1985).

Our first task was to determine what instrumentation already existed. Therefore, the literature on evaluating treatment environments in long-term care settings was reviewed. Nothing directly relevant to ADHC, as expressed in the VA program guidelines, was found. Therefore, existing instruments indirectly related to ADHC were used to develop the pilot instruments (Conrad, 1984; UCLA Department of Medicine, 1983; Moos and Lemke, 1984). Using these instruments, a preliminary draft of the ADHC instrumentation was developed and taken to collaborating clinical sites for their in-depth review of the clarity, format, and appropriateness of the forms and the items. This process resulted in a completed preliminary draft of the instruments. This draft was sent to the evaluation team for review. Site visits and discussions with ADHC providers led to further revisions. The resulting draft then went through another round of reviews by stakeholders and leaders in the field identified by the VA evaluation team and VA central office. It is important to note that the reviews concentrated on the elimination of items irrelevant to a medical or day hospital model of ADHC but included items relevant to this model.

*Measuring Philosophy, Structure, and Process.* As depicted in Table 3, the ADCAP is a quantitative assessment of six components of ADHC. These components assess the philosophy, structure, and process of the programs.

38

## Table 3.  The Content of the Adult Day Care Assessment Procedure

| Philosophy | Content | |
|---|---|---|
| Social Environment Scales (# of items) | Independence Promoting Approach (13) Family and Home Caregiver Involvement (5) Cohesiveness of Staff and Members (10) Organization (4) Teamwork (9) Leader and Member Interaction (8) Ecological Orientation of the Program (6) Behavioral Management; e.g., psychodynamic vs. behaviorist philosophy (16) Biophysical Treatment Approach (2) | |

**Means/Structure**

| Structural Features | Location Space and Facilities Bathrooms and Toilets | Equipment/Furniture Activity Areas Transportation |
|---|---|---|
| Policy and Program Information | Linkages with Other Organizations Program Auspices Staff Training Funding Sources | |
| Staffing Information | Volunteers and Students Core and Consulting Staff The Administrator (Fiedler, Bons, Hastings, 1975) | |

**Action/Process**

| Services and Activities | Hours of Operation Psychosocial Activities Recreational Activities Activities and Services for Clients' Families | Case Management Medical Services Self Care Activities |
|---|---|---|

**Population**

| Client and Caregiver Information | Discharge Information Client Description | |
|---|---|---|

Additionally, as Figure 2 illustrates, the appropriate delivery of services is dependent on the selection, enrollment, and participation of the target population. In the VA evaluation all patients are administered an extensive battery of physical, functional, and psychological assessments that will also serve, on subsequent administrations, as the outcome measures. The ADCAP provides a program level assessment of clients and home caregivers.

*Program Development and Improvement.* The availability of these instruments has important implications for the implementation and evaluation of ADHC projects. As the foregoing description indicates, the

ADCAP was designed primarily to serve a measurement function in evaluating ADHC. However, this set of instruments also constitutes a set of statements about the important elements of ADHC in general. In other words, they not only measure program philosophy but they also serve as guidelines for its implementation. Using these statements it is possible to develop norms or quality standards for the ADHC on the measured elements. Thereby, the ADCAP can play an active role in the development of ADHC in the VA. Further work in establishing the reliability and validity of the ADCAP will be performed under a grant from the American Association of Retired Persons Andrus Foundation (Conrad and Hughes, 1986).

### Recommendations and Conclusion

Program developers commonly write program philosophies. However, most are not written very well. One reason is that this skill is not taught, emphasized, or, perhaps, known. Guidelines for composing program philosophies should be developed.

Assessing the congruence between the program philosophy and the resources, project norms, and target populations means having accurate measures of these components and employing statistical methods that enable an assessment of the degree of congruence (Roberts-Gray, 1985; Moos and Lemke, 1984). A better understanding of which elements should be congruent, the strength of the congruence, and the appropriate statistical methods to be used in assessing congruence is necessary. The ability to measure enables the setting of standards that promote program improvement before summative evaluation takes place. Additionally, these measures and methods should be utilized more often in program evaluations because they enable the explanation of outcomes while indicating how those outcomes can be improved.

Because of space limitations, we were not able to demonstrate methods for examining the relative efficacy of program elements in effecting outcomes. Unfortunately, there is very little literature to which to refer to illustrate these methods. Readers may refer to Conrad (1983) or write the first author for a demonstration and discussion of basic causal modeling techniques in testing program philosophy.

It seems to us that within a program it is proper to define a program philosophy—the values (standards, methods, and goals) and the theories (for example, psychological, biomedical) of the program. Once a set of program philosophies is defined, it will be possible to combine individual program philosophies into classes. Once we are able to classify program philosophies, we will be able to make general statements about which classes of philosophies are useful in accomplishing certain classes of goals. When we are able to do this, we will have program theory.

**40**

## References

Apter, S. J. *Troubled Children/Troubled Systems*. Elmsford, N.Y.: Pergamon Press, 1982.

Bickman, L. "Improving Established Statewide Programs: A Component Theory of Evaluation." *Evaluation Review*, 1985, *9*, 189-208.

Brickman, P., Rabinowitz, V. C., Karuza, J., Jr., Coates, D., Cohn, E., and Kidder, L. "Models of Helping and Coping." *American Psychologist*, 1982, *37*, 368-384.

Brown, G., and Palmer, D. "A Review of BEH Funded Personnel Preparation Programs in Emotional Disturbance." *Exceptional Children*, 1977, *44*, 168-175.

Campbell, D. T., and Erlebacher, A. "How Regression Artifacts in Quasi-Experimental Evaluations Can Mistakenly Make Compensatory Education Look Harmful." In J. Hellmuth (ed.), *Compensatory Education: A National Debate*. Vol. 3. *Disadvantaged Child*. New York: Brunner-Mazel, 1970.

Campbell, D. T., and Stanley, J. C. "Experimental and Quasi-Experimental Designs for Research and Teaching." In N. L. Gage (ed.), *Handbook of Research on Teaching*. Skokie, Ill.: Rand McNally, 1963.

Chen, H.-T., and Rossi, P. H. "Evaluating with Sense: The Theory-Driven Approach." *Evaluation Review*, 1983, *7*, 283-302.

Conrad, K. J. "A Demonstration of Causal Modeling in the Utilization of Program Implementation Measures." Paper presented at the annual meeting of the American Educational Research Association, Montreal, 1983. (ERIC Document Reproduction Service No. ED 229 394)

Conrad, K. J. "The Geriatric Evaluation Unit Questionnaire." Unpublished instrument, Medical District 17, Health Services Research and Development Center, Hines Veterans Administration Hospital, Hines, Ill., 1984.

Conrad, K. J., and Eash, M. J. "Measuring Implementation and Multiple Outcomes in a Child-Parent Center Compensatory Education Program." *American Educational Research Journal*, 1983, *20*, 221-236.

Conrad, K. J., Eash, M. J., and Schevers, T. J. "The Effects of PL 94-142 on School Services to Adolescents with Behavior Disorders." Paper presented at the annual meeting of the American Educational Research Association, New Orleans, 1984.

Conrad, K. J., and Hughes, S. L. "Assessing the Structures, Populations, and Processes of Adult Day Care Programs." Proposal funded by the American Association of Retired Persons Andrus Foundation to Northwestern University, 1986.

Conrad, K. J., Rothman, M. L., and Miller, T. Q. "Assessing the Structures and Processes of the Adult Day Health Care Program." Technical report #85-016. Medical District 17, Health Services Research and Development Field Program, Veterans Administration Hospital, Hines, Ill., 1985.

Cook, T. D., and Campbell, D. T. *Quasi-Experimentation: Design and Analysis Issues for Field Settings*. Skokie, Ill.: Rand McNally, 1979.

Cook, T. D., Leviton, L. C., and Shadish, W. R., Jr. "Program Evaluation." In G. Lindzey and E. Aronson (eds.), *The Handbook of Social Psychology*. (3rd ed.) New York: Random House, 1985.

Cooley, W. W., and Lohnes, P. R. *Evaluation Research in Education*. New York: Irvington, 1974.

*Estate of Smith* v. *M. Heckler*. *Federal Reporter*, 2nd Series, 747. St. Paul, Minn.: West, 1984.

Ezrahi, Y. "Political Contexts of Science Indicators." In Y. Elkana and others (eds.), *Toward a Metric of Science Indicators*. New York: Wiley-Interscience, 1978.

Hackman, J. R., and Morris, G. G. "Group Processes and Group Effectiveness: A

Reappraisal." In L. Berkowitz (ed.), *Group Processes*. Orlando, Fla.: Academic Press, 1975.

Haney, W. *The Follow Through Planned Variation Experiment*. Vol. 5: *A Technical History of the National Follow Through Evaluation*. Cambridge, Mass.: The Huron Institute, 1977.

Hare, A. P. "A Functional Interpretation of Interaction." In H. H. Blumberg, A. P. Hare, V. Kent, and M. Davies (eds.), *Small Groups and Social Interaction*. Vol. 2. New York: Wiley, 1983.

Hedrick, S. C., Inui, T. S., Rothman, M. L., and Watts, C. A. "Evaluation of Effectiveness and Costs of Adult Day Health Care." Proposal under review at Veterans Administration Health Services Research and Development Service. HSR&D Field Program, American Lake Veterans Administration Medical Center, Tacoma, Wash., 1984.

Judd, C. M., and Kenny, D. A. "Process Analysis." *Evaluation Review*, 1981, *5*, 602-619.

Lemke, S., and Moos, R. H. "Assessing the Institutional Policies of Sheltered Care Settings." *Journal of Gerontology*, 1980, *35*, 96-107.

Lemke, S., and Moos, R. H. "Quality of Residential Settings for Elderly Adults." *Journal of Gerontology*, 1986, *41*, 268-276.

Linn, M. W., Gurel, L., and Linn, B. S. "Patient Outcomes as a Measure of Quality of Nursing Home Care." *Amer. Journal of Public Health*, 1977, *67*, 337-342.

McDaniels, G. L. "The Evaluation of Follow Through." *Educational Researcher*, 1975, *4*, 7-11.

McGrath, J. E. *Groups: Interaction and Performance*. Englewood Cliffs, N.J.: Prentice-Hall, 1984.

McGrath, J. E., and Kravitz, D. A. "Group Research." *Annual Review of Psychology*, 1982, *33*, 195-230.

Medley, D. M., and Mitzel, H. E. "A Technique for Measuring Classroom Behavior." *Journal of Educational Psychology*, 1958, *49*, 86-92.

Moos, R. *Evaluating Treatment Environments: A Social Ecological Approach*. New York: Wiley, 1974.

Moos, R. H. "Specialized Living Environments for Older People: A Conceptual Framework for Evaluation." *Journal of Social Issues*, 1980, *36*, 75-95.

Moos, R., and Lemke, S. *Multiphasic Environmental Assessment Procedure (MEAP)*. Stanford, Calif.: Palo Alto Social Ecology Laboratory, Veterans Administration Medical Center and Stanford University, 1984.

Morse, W. C., Smith, J. M., and Acker, N. *Videotape Training Packages in Child Variance. The Ecological Approach: A Self-Instructional Module*. Mimeo. Ann Arbor: University of Michigan, School of Education, 1978.

Parsons, T. *Structure and Process in Modern Societies*. New York: Free Press, 1960.

Pressman, J. L., and Wildavsky, A. B. *Implementation*. Berkeley: University of California Press, 1973.

Quay, H. C. "The Three Faces of Evaluation: What Can Be Expected to Work." In L. Sechrest, S. G. West, M. A. Phillips, R. Redner, and W. Keaton (eds.), *Evaluation Studies Review Annual*. Vol. 4. Beverly Hills, Calif.: Sage, 1979.

Revelle, W. "Hierarchical Cluster Analysis and the Internal Structure of Tests." *Multivariate Behavioral Research*, 1979, *14*, 57-74.

Rezmovic, E. L. "Assessing Treatment Implementation Amid the Slings and Arrows of Reality." *Evaluation Review*, 1984, *8*, 187-204.

Roberts-Gray, C. "Managing the Implementation of Innovators." *Evaluation and Program Planning*, 1985, *8*, 261-269.

Rokeach, M. *Beliefs, Attitudes, and Values: A Theory of Organization and Change.* San Francisco: Jossey-Bass, 1968.

Sabatino, D. A., and Mauser, A. J. *Intervention Strategies for Specialized Secondary Education.* Boston: Allyn & Bacon, 1978.

Scheirer, M. A., and Rezmovic, E. L. "Measuring the Degree of Program Implementation: A Methodological Review." *Evaluation Review,* 1983, 7, 599–633.

Stake, R. E. "The Countenance of Educational Evaluation." *Teachers College Record,* 1967, 68, 523–540.

Tuckman, B. W. "Developmental Sequence in Small Groups." *Psychological Bulletin,* 1965, 63, 384–399.

Tyler, R. W. *Basic Principles of Curriculum and Instruction.* Chicago: University of Chicago Press, 1950.

UCLA Department of Medicine. *The Structure of Primary Care Practice: An Inventory.* Los Angeles: University of California–Los Angeles Department of Medicine, 1983.

Veterans Administration. Draft ADHC program guidelines, Washington, D. C.: Geriatrics and Extended Care, Veterans Administration, 1984.

Westinghouse Learning Corporation/Ohio University. *The Impact of Head Start: An Evaluation of the Effects of Head Start on Children's Cognitive and Affective Development.* Washington, D.C.: Office of Economic Opportunity, 1969.

Wholey, J. S. *Evaluation: Promise and Performance.* Washington, D.C.: Urban Institute, 1979.

Worthen, B. R., and Sanders, J. R. *Educational Evaluation: Theory and Practice.* Belmont, Calif.: Wadsworth, 1973.

*Kendon J. Conrad is senior research associate at the Center for Health Services and Policy Research, Northwestern University, and for the Health Systems Research and Development field program, Veterans Administration Hospital, Hines, Illinois.*

*Todd Q. Miller is research assistant for the Health Systems Research and Development field program, Veterans Administration Hospital, and a graduate student at Loyola University, Chicago.*

*Two types of program theory tools—conceptual and action heuristics—can help evaluators improve programs by expanding conceptions of problems and solutions and by narrowing the focus of decision alternatives for action.*

# Conceptual and Action Heuristics: Tools for the Evaluator

*Charles McClintock*

The main objective of a formative strategy of evaluation is to stimulate decision making that will improve program performance. Program theory, that is those concepts that are used to explain how a program or its implementation will work, plays an important role in decision making, since it can be used to both expand conceptions of problems and solutions and to narrow attention on a manageable set of action alternatives. The purpose of this chapter is to describe a set of techniques for complicating and simplifying program theory, referred to as conceptual and action heuristics, that can be used to identify the significant concepts and action alternatives in policy and program development. This is an important activity, since creative and systematic techniques for concept and action formulation are scarce compared with the range of traditional analytic methods for answering questions about program outcomes (Leavitt, 1976; Alexander, 1979). This review of conceptual and action heuristics is drawn from literature on

The author would like to thank Leonard Bickman, Jennifer Greene, Jules Marquart, Charles Nocera, William Trochim, and an anonymous reviewer for providing helpful comments.

L. Bickman (ed.). *Using Program Theory in Evaluation.*
New Directions for Program Evaluation, no. 33. San Francisco: Jossey-Bass, Spring 1987.

measurement and evaluation, organizational behavior and development, and learning theory. The eclectic nature of this collection highlights the varied roles (methodologist, change agent, educator) and settings (profit and nonprofit) in which evaluators may work.

## Formative Evaluation and Uncertainty

The approach to formative evaluation used here is based on a concept of organizational learning that requires the evaluator to (1) work with program stakeholders to increase uncertainty about program structure by exploring alternative strategies and organizational arrangements for defining problems and delivering services, and (2) reduce uncertainty about levels of program performance, such as service activities, short-term effects, and costs (McClintock, 1984). Conceptual and action heuristics reflect these purposes respectively, although the difference between the two types of evaluation tools is mainly one of emphasis and the particular application (see Table 1).

A heuristic is a method for problem solving or learning. Heuristics for conceptualizing are used to increase uncertainty by expanding the domain of thinking about concepts and their interrelationships. Wicker (1985), for example, describes an approach to expanding conceptual frameworks. He advises that one should (1) play with ideas (for example, by using metaphors), (2) consider contexts (for example, by making comparisons with problems from other settings), (3) question assumptions (for example, by treating assumptions as both true and false under different conditions), and (4) systematize conceptual frameworks (for example, by specifying the relationships among concepts).

Organizational learning and program improvement require experimentation in action in addition to conceptual development. In contrast to the expansion dynamic in conceptualizing, the real world of administrative action often requires reducing uncertainty through simplification and contraction of alternatives in order to manage the cognitive demands of choice. An example of an action heuristic is the Delphi technique when it is used to converge on ideas, priorities, or estimates about problems and programs that have greatest plausibility and credence for a group (Delbec and Van de Ven, 1971).

Some heuristics may be used for expansion and convergence. Maynard-Moody and McClintock (forthcoming) describe how organizational goals function to create variability and stability. They argue that goal setting and implementing activities produce variability in conceptions of program purpose and direction, while goal enforcing and evaluating can be used to narrow attention and motivate action.

The use of conceptual and action heuristics to increase or decrease uncertainty highlights the role of heuristics in developing program theory.

### Table 1. Summary of Conceptual and Action Heuristics and Their Applications as Formative Evaluation Tools

| Heuristic | Applications as a Formative Evaluation Tool |
| --- | --- |
| A. Conceptual | Increase uncertainty about program structure and organizational arrangements by surfacing new and conflicting conceptualizations for problems and solutions; stimulate thinking. |
| 1. Analysis of Metaphors | Identify generative metaphors and resolve conceptual conflicts. |
| 2. Concept Development | Visualize similarities and differences in stakeholders' conceptual domains. |
| 3. Relational Analysis | Explore bivariate relationships among concepts. |
| 4. Mapping Sentences/ Concept Maps | Explore multivariate relationships among concepts. |
| B. Action | Decrease uncertainty about program performance by clarifying program activities, short-term effects and costs; stimulate action. |
| 1. Evaluability, Implementation and Component Assessments | Identify scope of program outcomes and identify possible interventions to change causal relationships. |
| 2. Causal Models and Maps | Simulate program outcomes and identify possible interventions to change causal relationships. |
| 3. Decision and Cost-Benefit Analysis | Identify specific decision paths and estimate expected costs and benefits. |

As Bickman (this volume) indicates, improved program theory is helpful in designing evaluations. The process of explicating theory, however, is itself a useful type of formative evaluation. The use of conceptual and action heuristics in this process deemphasizes the measurement of program outcomes and highlights what every seasoned practitioner knows: Framing questions in creative ways takes one at least half the distance toward useful answers.

Program theory is influenced by various processes including: political and legislative maneuvering (Redman, 1973), the application of social science knowledge and research methods for policy analysis (Shotland and Mark, 1985), governmental and community dynamics of implementation (Pressman and Wildavsky, 1973), and the behavior of human service managers and professionals in providing services to clients (Lipsky, 1980). The conceptual and action heuristics described here are presented as methods for developing program theory at the level of program management and service delivery. They are less likely to be applicable at the macro level than are tactics of legislative maneuvering, bargaining, and bureaucratic or political power (see Shadish, this volume).

## Conceptual Heuristics

The discussion of conceptual heuristics moves from the analysis of metaphors to procedures for graphically portraying problem/program concepts and their relationships. The purpose of conceptual heuristics is to elucidate the subjective program theories held by various program stakeholders; the definitions of the situations that underlie the choices and commitments these stakeholders make.

*Analyzing Metaphors.* A useful starting point for understanding the implicit concepts that underlie program theory is the analysis of metaphors. Schön (1979) and House (1983) have argued that metaphoric thinking is important as a cognitive basis for how we generate or frame our definitions of social problems and programs. For example, Schön describes the historical view of urban slums in which the communities were defined as marginal and diseased. As a result, programs were designed to raze and replace communities in the belief that this renovation would help eradicate the "disease" of slum conditions. An alternative perspective is provided by Perlman (1976), who portrays urban squatter settlements in Brazil (the *favelos*) as healthy communities of cultural vitality comparable to the larger population. Their very existence and persistence under conditions of discrimination in access to resources is taken as evidence of the strength of the *favela* culture. The programmatic approach to a "healthy" slum is one in which discrimination barriers are removed and the existing culture is supported by the larger community.

Metaphors are scattered throughout anecdotes of social problems. Often they are only implicit in conversation and formal argument, and they thus must be inferred through content analysis. Through such an analysis of a leading text in program evaluation (Rossi, Freeman, and Wright, 1979), House (1983) argues that a common metaphor for social problems is that of the target. Correspondingly, social programs are characterized as machines, assembly lines, and conduits through which targets are impacted.

These metaphors are all instrumental in nature. They refer to processes that have a means-ends relationship and are grounded in purposive rationality (Satow, 1975). Other metaphors for social problems are possible. By taking a value-rational approach in which ideologies govern the worth of activities, we might view social problems as opportunities to engage in acts of charity, love, or altruism. Social programs then can be characterized as expressions of compassionate feelings or positive cultural values. An example of program theory grounded in this kind of metaphor is described by Lerman (1968). He reviewed evaluations of residential treatment programs for juvenile delinquents and consistently found that the programs did not have lower rates of recidivism when compared with several harsher control conditions including incarceration. From the perspective of the industrial/target metaphors, the program did not have the desired impact. Lerman argues, however, that despite the absence of effectiveness results, the residential programs should be continued, since they expressed humanitarian values and could not be shown to have done harm to their residents or to recidivism rates in comparison with the control group alternatives.

It would be useful for the evaluator to surface conflicting metaphors, for example programs as tools versus programs as expressions, prior to an assessment of solutions. Indeed, the clarification of these different metaphors and their implications for program design and criteria of effectiveness would, in itself, constitute a useful exercise in formative evaluation.

Schön (1979) claims that conceptual conflicts based on competing generative metaphors are "often unresolvable by appeal to the facts" (p. 269). Thus, the evaluator is faced with the task of creating new concepts (metaphors or otherwise) that might allow for some constructive compromise between antithetical views. Basically, the process of integrating metaphors involves four steps: (1) attending to new aspects of the problem (slums are healthy and unhealthy), (2) renaming (a service is an act of caring), (3) regrouping and reordering features (services that express positive social values, looking for harmful effects instead of goal attainment), and (4) redefining boundaries of the situation (removal of access barriers, use of natural networks of helping).

It is difficult to describe in this brief presentation the linguistic and textual analysis techniques that evaluators might use for the analysis of metaphors. Useful examples may be found, however, in Reddy's (1979) analysis of communication metaphors, Packer's (1985) comparison of hermeneutic inquiry with traditional social science methods, and the work of Schön (1979) and House (1983). In many instances, the procedures are similar to content analysis in which thematic codes are developed from verbal and textual data.

Although the analysis of metaphors proceeds from linguistic and textual analysis, the evaluator's role often requires working with program stakeholders in a structured manner. The following techniques can be used for this kind of concept analysis.

*Clarifying Concepts.* Trochim (1985) describes a structured process for stimulating greater awareness of conceptual domains among program stakeholders. First, the selected stakeholders generate words, phrases, or sentences that have relevance to the program (for example, its goals, problems, satisfactions, processes). Second, through a sorting procedure, participants identify those descriptors that match. In each step the emphasis is on items and groupings that are meaningful for the participants. The evaluator then analyzes the sort results using multidimensional scaling and cluster analysis to produce a concept map that represents the locations and groupings of the original descriptors. Participants can observe graphic portrayals of the similarities and differences in their perceptions of the program. These graphs then become the refined raw material for further group discussion that is designed to educate participants about their conceptual understandings of the program, set priorities, design programs, or contribute information about problematic concepts.

Clarifying concepts and their degree of similarity is a heuristic for generating questions and new ideas, but it does not necessarily lead to a careful examination of the relationships among concepts. There are several techniques available to the formative evaluator using systematic analysis that can be used to identify the relational structure of program theories.

*Exploring Relationships.* Weick (1979) describes a procedure for discovering relationships among concepts based on Crovitz's (1970) analysis of domain (nouns) and relational (prepositions and conjunctions) language. Participants begin by writing a brief statement of an important problem. For example, one might write the following problem statement: "With declining rates of public expenditure for social programs, how can services be delivered to those in need?"

The next step is to identify all the nouns in the problem statement (declining expenditures, social programs, services, those in need) and write them on a circular piece of paper that will function as a base for a set of paper discs. The second disc, slightly smaller in diameter, contains the relational words (with, of, for, to, in), and the third and smallest disc has a duplicate set of domain words. By attaching the three discs at the center, it is possible to rotate them so that new relations between concepts can be explored.

For example, take the two domain concepts of services and those in need. Using a different set of relational words (Crovitz identifies forty-two in English) results in different ways of thinking about the problem:

- Services *after* those in need (suggesting that the administrative requirements of service delivery be attended to only after the clients are given attention)
- Services *by* those in need (the self-help concept)
- Services *over* those in need (protection of the service structure and its ideologies is more important than the temporary budgeting problems)
- Services *with* those in need (the sites and services model).

Obviously, there are arbitrary aspects of this linguistic relational analysis process. For example, one can reverse the direction of the relationship between domain terms. Thus, those in need *on* services suggests a kind of bottom up or adversarial pressure on the planning and service delivery process. The results of relational analysis will depend on which stakeholders are selected, how problem statements are formulated, and which domain terms receive most attention. Also, there is a tendency to focus on bivariate relationships within a single problem statement, when it might be more fruitful to examine the overlap of problems and their underlying multivariate structure.

*Mapping Sentences and Concept Maps.* Mapping sentences, a procedure based on Guttman's facet theory, are systematic verbal representations of clusters of variables and the relationships among them (Canter, 1985). The following example illustrates a mapping sentence that could serve as the beginning of an evaluative design:

The development of employer-sponsored family support programs for

$$\begin{bmatrix} \text{employee assistance} \\ \text{child care} \\ \text{career counseling} \\ \text{parental leave} \end{bmatrix} \begin{array}{l} \text{requires review of} \\ \text{personnel policies} \\ \text{regarding} \end{array} \begin{bmatrix} \text{flexible hours} \\ \text{leave} \\ \text{supervision} \\ \text{relocation assistance} \end{bmatrix}$$

which are dependent on employer concerns such as $\begin{bmatrix} \text{costs} \\ \text{equity} \\ \text{liability} \\ \text{productivity} \end{bmatrix}$ and the

needs of employees related to $\begin{bmatrix} \text{family life} \\ \text{personal development} \\ \text{career development} \end{bmatrix}$

To portray the structure of concepts and relationships in a manner that reflects spatial or process arrangements, the evaluator might create a pictorial display. Novak and Gowin (1984) have developed procedures for arranging concepts in hierarchical structures that display the variety of vertical and horizontal relationships within a program and between the program and its context. Concept maps can be developed at the individual level, or they can integrate the perceptions of different stakeholders. Concept maps are arranged hierarchically, with the more important and encompassing concepts arranged at the top and horizontal and vertical linkages defined verbally. This approach has several advantages. The hierarchical design reflects an important cognitive basis for learning complex conceptual structures. Verbal description of causal connections among concepts permits description of the variety of relationships that can exist (for example, direct, indirect, intermittent, cyclical, circular, logical, mathematical).

**Action Heuristics**

The purpose of exploring the conceptual underpinnings of social problems is to build an expanded understanding of how people evaluate the world and why they make choices about how to act; that is, to understand the complexity of human perceptions. Given this complexity, however, it is then necessary to have a set of heuristics that simplify reality in order to make possible deliberate choice and action (Rockart, 1979; Brunsson, 1982). With conceptual heuristics, program theory is expanded, questioned, and complicated. Action heuristics are used to simplify program theory so that decisions can be made about implementing, expanding, altering, or terminating specific programs or activities. Action heuristics are focused on specific interventions and their expected costs and benefits.

*Evaluability, Implementation, and Component Assessments.* It is often the case that administrators have little reliable information about the scope, content, and nature of client contacts related to the array of programs currently under their supervision (McClintock and Reilinger, 1980; Bickman, 1985). Such information is critically important before one can intervene to improve program implementation and performance (see Conrad and Miller, this volume; Scheirer, this volume).

Evaluability and implementation assessments share a common purpose in identifying which programs or program components are actually in place. Where gaps or problems are identified, the assessment procedures specify steps that help determine whether the barriers lie in program or implementation theory.

Bickman (1985) describes a more structured procedure derived from evaluability assessment that treats program components instead of entire programs as the units of analysis. The procedure can be used for one or more of the following purposes: description of the scope of program activity, identification of service gaps and overlaps, and evaluation of quality. The component procedure involves the following steps: (1) list and refine program components from existing data on program sites, literature, and expert opinion; (2) develop a questionnaire about significant activities under each component that provides descriptive data on the type and extent of implementation; (3) develop and score weighted measures of component quality based on expert judgment; and (4) compare the quality ratings of selected components with field tests of effectiveness.

The result of each of these assessment procedures is to set priorities for action based on what is known about the source of the problem (program theory or implementation barrier) and the need for, extent, or quality of current program activity. It may be necessary, however, to be more specific about the causal structure of programs or activities prior to taking action. Causal modeling can stimulate action by clarifying expected relationships among program components.

*Causal Modeling.* The use of models to simplify the dynamics of complex systems is a widespread tool in policy analysis (Richardson, 1984). Some of the conceptual heuristics described earlier are simple forms of modeling. Used as an action heuristic, causal modeling is a method for stimulating alternative policy and program decisions. Causal simulations vary in terms of the nature of their inputs (data, judgments), complexity of operation (verbal, mathematical), the form of their outputs (mathematical, graphic), and type of use (stimulate decisions on policies and specific interventions, guide further monitoring and research). The process of developing and using causal simulations is at least as important as their outcomes, since it forces one to be explicit about program theory.

If the evaluator is making specific recommendations for change in the support and delivery of services, it may be useful to develop maps of causal relations among variables to facilitate visual understanding of action alternatives. The techniques for creating causal maps vary from those based on verbalizations and visual displays (Roos and Hall, 1980) to valency matrices in which stakeholders identify the existence of causal linkages between each combination of variables and the nature of those linkages (zero, positive, negative relationships) (Axelrod, 1976).

In the context of formative evaluation, the former approach is more likely, since it generally provides more flexibility for quick visual manipulation of map structures. For example, Eden, Jones, and Sims (1983) describe a sequence of steps that can be used to map the varying ideas about causal relations among program variables for a group of stakeholders and to verify which causal loops are actually producing unintended and undesired effects. The process begins with identification of the concepts and elements that are thought to be part of the problem domain. This is done through interviews on a selected subject (for example, health care costs), identification of the central problematic events (cost of health care, recidivism, decline in inpatient/outpatient ratio), and attribution of the causes or explanations for these events (defensive medicine, unemployment, restrictions of third-party payments). Connecting lines are drawn between concepts that are causally related, and a plus or minus sign is given to each line to represent positive or negative linear correlations.

Figure 1 portrays a simple causal map of a problem in health care costs. By completing this process in a small group, it is possible to judge the degree of similarity among individual causal maps and of the interdependence of the problems represented. As discussion proceeds, some variables may be collapsed while others are differentiated into more than one factor. Causal relations can shift, and reciprocal causalities between two variables may emerge.

Of greater concern than the methods for development is how causal maps can be used as action heuristics. If one consolidated map does not emerge, it is necessary to highlight contrasting causes for a given problem

**Figure 1. Example of a Deviation-Amplifying Causal Map**

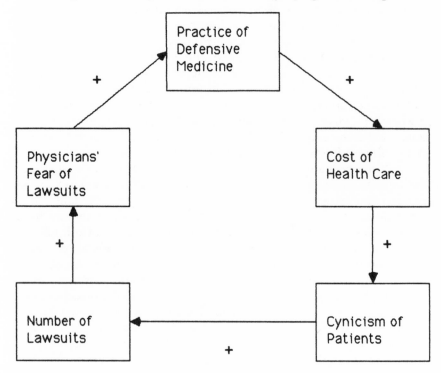

(physician's fear of lawsuits, number of lawsuits), or different perceptions of important outcomes (cost of health care versus defensive medicine). This activity will focus attention on specific action alternatives. Alternatively, one can gather evidence that will permit the group to simulate some or all of the causal loops in the map. Typically, however, not all variables can be quantified, because adequate operational indicators cannot be agreed on or because reliable data are not available. In some cases it may be possible to specify threshold levels or probabilistic relationships. For example, the following questions could be asked: The current rate of lawsuits is x per year. What would be an acceptable rate? If this were achieved what reduction would be seen in the level of defensive medicine? What is the next feasible reduction in lawsuits and what reduction in defensive medicine would that produce? Whichever approach is taken, Eden, Jones, and Sims (1983) have developed microcomputer software to process the information in the maps, to group variables that have an influence on key concepts, to compare and merge maps of different stakeholders, and to explore alternative parameter and relationship assumptions.

Causal maps have other features that can be used to analyze action alternatives. First, elements that have arrows outgoing from them are independent variables, while those with incoming arrows are dependent variables. The elements with incoming and outgoing arrows are interdependent variables, and they have special significance due to their multiple causal connections. By summing the direct (A → B, B → C) and indirect (A → C) causal connections, it is possible to identify those variables and relationships that will have the greatest potential impact from a policy or program intervention. Similarly, for maps that are developed from matrix comparisons of variables, the evaluator can derive reachability matrices (which show all direct and indirect connections) and adjacency matrices (which identify the number of causal steps that exist between any two variables). Analysis of these matrices allows one to assess the total impact from manipulation of individual variables.

Second, starting with any interdependent variable, it is possible to identify causal loops—chains of causal connections that recycle back to a point of origin. There are two kinds of causal loops: those that spiral in a single direction (deviation-amplifying loops, which have an even number of negative signs) and those that are self-correcting (deviation-counteracting loops, which have an odd number of negative signs). When deviation-amplifying loops lead to undesired results, they constitute vicious circles of causal interactions that can only be altered by an intervention or eventually by destruction of the system. An example of a vicious circle is shown in Figure 1.

Finally, Weick (1979, pp. 85–86) lists several action strategies based on analysis of causal maps:

1. Reverse the causal direction between two variables: The number of lawsuits causes the level of patient cynicism.
2. Change the sign of a causal relationship: An increase in the number of lawsuits decreases physician fear.
3. Interrupt causality: Physician fear has no effect on defensive medicine.
4. Create variability in the direction of the relationship: Sometimes cynical patients file lawsuits, but as the number of lawsuits increases, patient cynicism is assuaged.
5. Remove a variable: Prohibit lawsuits against physicians.
6. Intensify or moderate a relationship: The practice of defensive medicine immediately leads to a significant increase in the cost of health care or, because of new cost containment regulations, has only a modest effect on costs.
7. Create another causal relationship that nullifies an undesirable effect: The number of lawsuits triggers a limit on the size of awards, which reduces physician fear.

8. Establish curvilinear relationships: Cynicism leads to lawsuits to the point where they become burdensome to patients, which leads to a search for alternative forms of care and a decline in lawsuits.

The plausibility and effectiveness of these actions will be determined by other factors in the situation. At the least, however, this is a procedure for creating action alternatives that frees one from the typical administrative dilemma of having too few solutions for an endless supply of unanticipated problems. After a set of solutions has been narrowed to those that are feasible, it is necessary to focus on the specific decision paths that will lead to the desired outcome.

*Decision and Cost-Benefit Analysis.* Decision analysis requires the evaluator to decompose a decision problem into separate choices, assess the role of chance (or imperfect correlation) and acceptable risk, calculate the effects of a sequence of interdependent choices, and assign cost and benefit values to the possible outcomes. This kind of analysis can be portrayed visually in decision trees, which show the outcome paths for each of a set of choices about program or activity alternatives (Stokey and Zeckhauser, 1978).

The following simple decision tree illustrates the idea where one alternative can benefit from matching funds from private donors.

| | | |
|---|---|---|
| | 80 percent chance of receiving matching funds | Total Allocated Cost $1,200 |
| Implement Program A | 20 percent chance of not receiving matching funds | Total Allocated Cost $2,400 |
| Implement Program B | | Total Allocated Cost $1,900 |

By calculating the expected monetary value of each alternative, this heuristic would lead to a choice of Program A [$EMV_A = 0.8(\$1,200) + 0.2(\$2,400) = \$1,440$] owing to its lower expected cost.

Many administrators do not have the luxury of choosing among alternative programs. Instead they must live with a given program but focus on how to reduce its ineffectiveness. Building on the logic of decision analysis, Cameron (1984) describes how to create fault trees, which provide a similar graphic portrayal of a sequence of actions that can be taken to improve the fault points in a series of interrelated program components.

The effectiveness of decision analysis rests on reasonable estimates of costs and benefits. Although such analyses are appealing theoretically, they are rarely used in the real world of program development owing to the difficulties of calculating precise values for costs and benefits (Levin,

1983; Smith and Smith, 1985). In addition to the complexity and expense of a thorough cost-benefit analysis, it is usually the case that due to political considerations, decision makers do not have the freedom to choose a program alternative just because of its appealing cost-benefit profile. Still, it is desirable to base administrative action on analysis that shows whether the anticipated benefits will equal or exceed estimated costs.

Two action heuristics that can clarify the cost-benefit question are based on judgmental evidence from stakeholders about whether or not benefits are likely to exceed costs. First, Nagel (1985) describes a procedure consisting of paired comparisons between nonmonetary program benefits and varying dollar values. By repeated comparisons at different dollar amounts, one can identify a turning point at which the nonmonetary benefits are valued less than the number of dollars. The procedure avoids the burdensome and tenuous assignment of absolute precise values for nonmonetized outcomes and instead focuses on the relative trade-offs between costs and benefits.

It is likely that different stakeholders will produce varying turning-point values. This is not a problem, however, if all values are above the estimated cost of the program. Boudreau (1984) emphasizes this point in his description of break-even analysis, which is based on a comparison of per person program costs and benefits. By graphing the estimated costs against varying levels of estimated benefits, one finds the point at which the program breaks even. It does not matter if there are large differences among the monetized estimates of program benefits gathered from stakeholders as long as these differences are clearly above or below the break-even point. If monetized benefits are not feasible, it is possible to use scaled judgments of program benefits similar to cost-effectiveness analysis. If the level of program benefits are judged by stakeholders to be above the break-even value, then one can feel more comfortable taking action.

## Conclusion

The chapters in this volume attest to the need for clarifying and creatively using program theory for evaluation design and program improvement. A related need has been discussed in the general field of causal modeling. Forrester (1984) argues that a major limitation of econometric models is that they rely too heavily on numerical data bases. He proposes that effective models must also draw on mental data bases (the experiential evidence of observers) and written data bases (nonscientific literature). Conceptual and action heuristics represent tools for program development that, in addition to social science theory, directly draw on these sources of evidence. The exciting prospect for conceptual and action heuristics, along with other methods discussed in this volume, is that they stimulate interrelationships among the experiential, literary, and scientific bases of thought and action.

56

## References

Alexander, E. R. "The Design of Alternatives in Organizational Contexts: A Pilot Study." *Administrative Science Quarterly*, 1979, *24*, 382–404.

Axelrod, R. (ed.). *Structure of Decision: The Cognitive Maps of Political Elites.* Princeton, N.J.: Princeton University Press, 1976.

Bickman, L. "Improving Established Statewide Programs: A Component Theory of Evaluation." *Evaluation Review*, 1985, *9*, 189–208.

Boudreau, J. W. "Decision Theory Contributions to HRM Research and Practice." *Industrial Relations*, 1984, *23*, 198–217.

Brunsson, N. "The Irrationality of Action and Action Rationality: Decisions, Ideologies, and Organizational Actions." *Journal of Management Studies*, 1982, *19*, 29–44.

Cameron, K. "The Effectiveness of Ineffectiveness." In B. M. Staw and L. L. Cummings (eds.), *Research and Organizational Behavior.* Vol. 6. Greenwich, Conn.: JAI, 1984.

Canter, D. (ed.). *Facet Theory: Approaches to Social Research.* New York: Springer-Verlag, 1985.

Crovitz, H. F. *Galton's Walk.* New York: Harper & Row, 1970.

Delbec, A. L., and Van de Ven, A. H. "Problem Analysis and Program Design: Nominal Group Process Technique." *Journal of Applied Behavioral Science*, 1971, *7*, 466–492.

Eden, C., Jones, S., and Sims, D. *Messing About in Problems: An Informal Structured Approach to Their Identification and Management.* Elmsford, N.Y.: Pergamon, 1983.

Forrester, J. W. "Information Sources for Modeling the National Economy." In J. Richardson (ed.), *Models of Reality: Shaping Thought and Action.* Mt. Airy, Md.: Lomond, 1984.

House, E. R. (ed.). *Philosophy of Evaluation.* New Directions for Program Evaluation, no. 19. San Francisco: Jossey-Bass, 1983.

Leavitt, H. J. "On the Design Part of Organizational Design." In R. H. Kilmann, L. R. Pondy, and D. P. Slevan (eds.), *The Management of Organizational Design: Strategies and Implementation.* New York: North Holland, 1976.

Lerman, P. "Evaluative Studies of Institutions for Delinquents: Implications for Research and Social Policy." *Social Work*, 1968, *13*, 55–64.

Levin, H. M. *Cost Effectiveness: A Primer.* Beverly Hills, Calif.: Sage, 1983.

Lipsky, M. W. *Street-Level Bureaucracy: Dilemmas of the Individual in Public Service.* New York: Russell Sage Foundation, 1980.

McClintock, C. "Toward a Theory of Formative Program Evaluation." In D. Deshler (ed.), *Evaluation for Program Improvement.* New Directions for Continuing Education, no. 24. San Francisco: Jossey-Bass, 1984.

McClintock, C., and Reilinger, E. "The Best-Laid Plans: Theory and Practice in Social Service Planning." *The Urban and Social Change Review*, 1980, *13*, 21–28.

Maynard-Moody, S., and McClintock, C. "Weeding an Old Garden: Toward a New Understanding of Organizational Goals." *Administration and Society*, forthcoming.

Nagel, S. S. "Economic Transformations of Nonmonetary Benefits in Program Evaluation." In J. S. Catterall (ed.), *Economic Evaluation of Public Programs.* New Directions for Program Evaluation, no. 26. San Francisco: Jossey-Bass, 1985.

Novak, J. D., and Gowin, D. B. *Learning How to Learn.* Cambridge, England: Cambridge University Press, 1984.

Packer, M. J. "Hermeneutic Inquiry in the Study of Human Conduct." *American Psychologist*, 1985, *40*, 1081–1093.

Perlman, J. *The Myth of Marginality: Urban Poverty and Politics in Rio de Janeiro.* Berkeley: University of California Press, 1976.

Pressman, J. L., and Wildavsky, A. B. *Implementation.* Berkeley: University of California Press, 1973.

Reddy, M. J. "The Conduit Metaphor—A Case of Frame Conflict in Our Language About Language." In A. Ortony (ed.), *Metaphor and Thought.* Cambridge, England: Cambridge University Press, 1979.

Redman, E. *The Dance of Legislation.* New York: Simon & Schuster, 1973.

Richardson, J. *Models of Reality: Shaping Thought and Action.* Mt. Airy, Md.: Lomond, 1984.

Rockart, J. F. "Chief Executives Define Their Own Data Needs." *Harvard Business Review*, 1979, *57*, 81–93.

Roos, L. R., Jr., and Hall, R. I. "Influence Diagrams and Organizational Power." *Administrative Science Quarterly*, 1980, *25*, 57–71.

Rossi, P. H., Freeman, H. E., and Wright, S. R. *Evaluation: A Systematic Approach.* Beverly Hills, Calif.: Sage, 1979.

Satow, R. L. "Value-Rational Authority and Professional Organizations: Weber's Missing Type." *Administrative Science Quarterly*, 1975, *20*, 526–531.

Schön, D. A. "Generative Metaphor: A Perspective on Problem Setting in Social Policy." In A. Ortony (ed.), *Metaphor and Thought.* Cambridge, England: Cambridge University Press, 1979.

Shotland, R. L., and Mark, M. M. (eds.). *Social Science and Social Policy.* Beverly Hills, Calif.: Sage, 1985.

Smith, N. L., and Smith, J. K. "State-Level Evaluation Uses of Cost Analysis: A National Descriptive Survey." In J. S. Catterall (ed.), *Economic Evaluation of Public Programs.* New Directions for Program Evaluation, no. 26. San Francisco: Jossey-Bass, 1985.

Stokey, E., and Zeckhauser, R. *A Primer for Policy Analysis.* New York: Norton, 1978.

Trochim, W.M.K. "Pattern Matching, Validity, and Conceptualization in Program Evaluation." *Evaluation Review*, 1985, *9*, 575–604.

Weick, K. E. *The Social Psychology of Organizing.* Reading, Mass.: Addison-Wesley, 1979.

Wicker, A. W. "Getting Out of Our Conceptual Ruts: Strategies for Expanding Conceptual Frameworks." *American Psychologist*, 1985, *40*, 1094–1103.

*Charles McClintock is associate professor of Human Service Studies and assistant dean of the College of Human Ecology, Cornell University. His teaching and research are in the areas of program evaluation and information management in organizations.*

*Program theory and implementation process theory contribute,*
*respectively, to specifying the what and the why of program*
*delivery. This chapter suggests ways in which evaluators*
*should incorporate both into their data collection designs.*

# Program Theory and Implementation Theory: Implications for Evaluators

*Mary Ann Scheirer*

Sensible program evaluation depends on assumptions that a program was delivered to a set of intended recipients. Although this statement may appear to be so obvious as to be not worth stating, in reality it embodies a number of complexities that are at the heart of many difficulties in program evaluation. As the authors of this volume discuss quite eloquently, the nature of the program being evaluated is often implicit, unclear, or ambivalent in its reference to evidence for cause-and-effect relationships. Further, even if the intended program components can be well specified, whether or not they are delivered to appropriate recipients raises the complex issues of implementation accuracy and how to achieve it. Meeting both sets of assumptions simultaneously—well-specified program components and accurate implementation—is not often a very difficult task. Therefore, these critical tasks must not be assumed to occur but must be carefully studied in themselves. In essence, before a realistic design for

The preparation of this chapter was partially supported by Grant #DEO6895 from the National Institute of Dental Research. Valuable suggestions for revisions were made by Leonard Bickman, Charles McClintock, and C. James Scheirer.

assessing outcomes or effects can be carried out, prior attention should be placed on methods for assessing both program components and program implementation.

The data collection designs needed for investigating program components and program implementation can, in turn, be related to two bodies of theory: program theory and implementation process theory. Program theory illuminates the set of cause-and-effect relationships that provide the rationale for the nature of the treatment. Program theory should be used by evaluators to guide the development of measuring instruments to assess what program was delivered. Implementation process theory, in contrast, discusses variables governing the delivery mechanism itself. It helps illuminate why a program is or is not being delivered accurately and examines potential solutions for increasing the extent of program delivery. Thus, both types of theory have implications for evaluators' roles, since both suggest types of data that can clarify program operations.

This chapter discusses the types of data that can be derived from both types of theory in order to contribute to more comprehensive evaluation designs. An evaluation focus on outcomes alone is not only premature in most cases but also fails to provide information needed to advise interested stakeholders on changes desirable in the program. Program evaluators should usually begin by tentatively assuming a "muddy" program with uncertain delivery. Accordingly, the overall evaluation design should provide for measurement of what and how the program was delivered rather than focusing exclusively on outcomes. This chapter discusses these two relatively neglected aspects of evaluation: program theory helps to specify what the program is, while implementation process theory helps evaluators and program managers to understand why the program was or was not delivered as intended.

In any actual delivery situation, the content of the program and the idiosyncrasies of its delivery are likely to be very interrelated. The activities that constitute program delivery are part of the daily work lives of the front-line program personnel. Other aspects of their work situations and of their own personal characteristics are likely to be major reasons for the extent of program delivery accomplished by each front-line deliverer. The distinction, then, between program content and implementation process is an analytic distinction made by the researcher. Keeping these constructs separate analytically is essential for any program evaluation, in order to specify and measure *how much* of the program (or what program subtype) was actually delivered in each situation to be evaluated. The extent of program delivery must be measured rather than assumed.

As in any cross-disciplinary writing, key terms can have different meanings when used in different research traditions. Several such terms will be defined here to avoid ambiguous usage. The term *theory* refers to a systematic delineation of cause-and-effect relationships. Program theory is one or more sets of causal assumptions that provide the rationale for a program intervention. Such theory might be based simply on common-sense notions about the way the relevant actors behave. Preferably, it is derived from empirically based scientific study of the content domain for the program components being developed. For social interventions this is usually the social science-based theory within the program area, such as education, criminal justice, health delivery, and so forth.

The terms *program, intervention,* and *innovation* are used inter-changeably to avoid overuse of any of them. They all refer to the content of whatever is being evaluated, with the implicit assumption that this is a new activity within that organizational situation.

The term *implementation* generally refers to ways in which a pro-gram is actually carried out. It has two quite separate aspects, however, which are not always kept distinct. The extent of implementation means the degree to which the intended program is delivered as planned, includ-ing both the accuracy of each deliverer-recipient interaction and the scope of the numbers of recipients. Extent of implementation implies actual measurement of one or more variables. Implementation process theory, however, refers to the body of knowledge about cause-and-effect relation-ships that helps explain why an observed extent of implementation was achieved. Since most programs to be evaluated take place within some type of organization, implementation process theory draws heavily from the extensive theoretical and empirical work concerning how people inter-act within organizations. Implementation process analysis uses many var-iables to attempt to account for the extent of implementation.

### Using Program Theory to Assess Extent of Implementation

The nature of a program often differs depending on whose opinion is consulted. From the top-down or macroperspective of a federal agency or other funding source, a program may be simply a funding mechanism to stimulate or support a general type of activity. From a local perspective, particularly that of a content specialist designing an intervention, a pro-gram will more likely embody one or more specific activities oriented toward a perceived problem. Each perspective will result in quite different answers to the question "What is the program?" (see Berman, 1978). Adopt-ing a macro- or microperspective or both is therefore a crucial first step in deciding what program theories should be the basis for assessing the extent of implementation.

An example may clarify this distinction between the macro- and microperspectives. In the early 1970s the National Science Foundation (NSF) initiated its innovation centers program, which provided funding for university-based centers to stimulate the development of innovation and entrepreneurship (Colton, 1981; Scheirer and others, 1985). Beyond this general mission the NSF program did not articulate a specific set of activities or cause-and-effect relationships that should be carried out at the local level. Instead, the innovation centers program was, in effect, a comparison of program designs for observing how grantees articulated a specific set of activities for interrelating technical innovation and entrepreneurial business development.

Not surprisingly, the actual activities that were carried out at each innovation center varied enormously. Several centers focused on enrolled students and developed educational program components, using theoretical underpinnings as diverse as role modeling theory or a parameter analysis model of the invention process. Other centers concentrated their efforts on entrepreneurial development outside the university, again incorporating a wide variety of theoretical assumptions, namely, that the center was a central node in a network of assistance sources, the center fostered a community of mutually assisting entrepreneurs, or the center was an extension type business assistance service. In sum, this program had multiple theoretical bases underlying the activities of its various centers, while from the macroperspective (federal) it was primarily a funding mechanism that purposely encouraged such diversity. No single, unified program theory could have articulated all the causal relationships believed relevant by the actors involved.

Such differences in perspective are to be expected when one considers the variety of stakeholders with interests in each program (see Bryk, 1983; Mark and Shotland, 1985). Federal agency staff may be primarily interested in satisfying political constituencies (client groups, legislators, or lobbyists). Their major criteria of success may be to demonstrate equity of resource allocation across the country or positive subjective response from local levels rather than valid empirical evidence of positive program outcomes. At the local level program theory specifying cause-and-effect relationships *may* provide a real point of guidance for designing and testing program components. Alternately, other local stakeholders may bring to the program a variety of other interests, from perceived client needs to staff members' career advancement.

***Role of the Evaluator.*** Given the diversity of program theories likely to be wrapped up in one program, the appropriate roles for evaluators are somewhat amorphous. Clearly, a program evaluation design focused primarily on outcomes is likely to overlook the diversity of underlying program theories. The results from such a study are not likely to be useful, whether or not the findings show positive effects. If the findings are positive, the evaluator is unable to supply documentation on what specific program activities brought about the desirable outcomes. If the findings are neutral or negative or vary substantially across program sites, the evaluator is unable to analyze the reasons for the disappointing results. Lack of program effects may be due to inadequate extent of implementation, to differences among sites in critical features of program delivery, to an inadequate research design or unreliable data, or to more basic flaws in the logic of cause-and-effect relationships embodied in the program theories.

Thus, evaluators must invest a considerable effort in documenting the intended program descriptions in relation to underlying program theories. By using one or more of the techniques described in this volume for illuminating the program theories of key stakeholders, the evaluator can make explicit the range of ideas concerning intended program activities. Program theory, both implicit and explicit, should guide the evaluator in specifying the intended program components. In essence, to measure the extent of implementation, the evaluator must be able to specify the range of possible program components. Measuring whether or not the intended program components are actually delivered then provides data on the extent and types of program implementation.

Relevant program theory and methodology for assessing the extent of program implementation differs, depending on whether the evaluator is working from a federal or local perspective and whether the program components are articulated in advance or are left to be developed by the implementors. Yet, in each case the evaluator can draw from the wide range of social science data collection strategies. These include the use of existing documents; records from information systems; surveys using mail, telephone, or in-person techniques; open-ended interviews; direct observations; and/or the use of unobtrusive measures. The criteria for the choice of data collection techniques remain the same: to obtain the most valid and most reliable information possible, given constraints of budget, time, and feasibility of data collection strategies.

*Measuring Extent of Macroimplementation.* When working from the macroperspective, even describing the extent of program implementation will likely require an examination of the filtering of the program through multiple bureaucratic layers (see Williams, 1980; Elmore, 1982). The extensive literature on policy implementation provides substantial theoretical guidance here (Pressman and Wildavsky, 1973; Sabatier and Mazmanian, 1979). From this perspective the program treatment is a set of federal resources, guidelines, and other activities intended to influence other (usually local) organizations. For these program components the relevant program theory may be synonymous with macrolevel implementation theory, since specifying the program's activities involves describing the bureaucratic activities linking federal and local levels. While the program may be rationalized in terms of ultimate effects on a set of assumed beneficiaries, the more immediate intent of the federal sponsor is likely to focus on meeting the needs of constituent organizations for stable funding, for regulations they deem appropriate, and so forth. Therefore, measuring the extent of implementation from the federal perspective should focus on the actual linking mechanisms between the levels involved.

Program description from this federal perspective involves examining the chain of effects (Yin, Quick, Bateman, and Marks, 1979) by which the program is translated from one level to another. Key analytic questions will be the following: How is the program described by various participants? What did actors at each bureaucratic level do to carry out or hamper the delivery of the program at the next level? Who was involved in this implementation process? Who became the participants or beneficiaries at the next level? What is the intent of the federal actors for actions at lower levels? Such questions are needed to describe what the program is, behaviorally, at each participating level and whether a unified set of outcome measures can capture its intended effects.

A major theme of this perspective is that program objectives are often interpreted differently by those at the various levels of an implementation chain, for example, several layers of a federal agency, or officials at federal, state, and local levels of a funding mechanism. Evaluation of the program usually requires a suspension of judgment concerning the real objectives of the program. Instead, careful attention is needed to what program behaviors were carried out at each level, what program theories they embody, and whether the diversity of objectives are compatible or conflicting.

If, as sometimes happens, explicit administrative standards are created at the start of a program concerning the details of program management at several participating levels, these standards might be used by the evaluator as a set of criteria against which to assess implementation performance. Even in this case, the a priori standards may not encompass the interests of many participants in the program. Frequently, however, it is not possible to specify in advance exactly what should be done by various administrators. In this case, the evaluator's role is to carefully document what is (or was) done during program administration and, usually, to relay to program staff the resulting observations about actual program components, problem areas, and potentially conflicting implicit theories. Analytically, data from these program process components can be related empirically to other measures, such as the efficiency or effectiveness of program delivery. This distinction between evaluating against a priori standards (an accounting approach) versus evaluating to address cause-and-effect relationships was well articulated in a recent article by the head of the program evaluation unit within the U.S. government's General Accounting Office (Chelimsky, 1985).

*Measuring Microimplementation.* The roles for an evaluator in describing the extent of program implementation at the local level are quite different from measuring macroimplementation. Here the evaluator's aim should be to collect data on each component of the program as delivered. When planning how to do this, the nature of the program or technology is crucial. Some interventions have been fully specified and tested for efficacy under controlled conditions, in advance of their local widespread implementation. For example, most medical regimens, education programs disseminated through the National Diffusion Network, and research-based mental health programs have undergone such development and testing. These programs usually have an explicit theoretical basis related to a set of recommended components, or activities, to be carried out by those who actually deliver the program. Other programs and innovations—for example, much health-related equipment, the use of computers for many applications, and developmental funding programs such as innovation centers—do not carry with them a fully developed set of components. Instead, the specific activities are left to be designed by the user. Consequently, such interventions frequently have a variety of program theories requiring that diverse component activities be carried out in many different ways.

When innovation specifications have been created during the development stages, the evaluator's role is to measure the degree to which the specifications are implemented in each delivery site involved in the evaluation. In this case, the program components should be articulated as a set of observable behaviors, which operationalize the program theory and provide the standard of accurate implementation. One study that used this approach for studying new adoptions of programs that had been validated by the National Diffusion Network (education) and the Exemplary Projects Program (criminal justice) found that the programs could each be described in terms of twenty to forty observable components (Blakely and others, 1984). Each component was scored on a scale of ideal, acceptable, and unacceptable performance, with an additive summary score calculated as the index of the extent of implementation for each adopter site in the study. These investigators also found that data collected by telephone interviews where program staff asked about these components were reasonably highly correlated with data gathered in on-site interviews and inspection of a subsample of sites. These findings suggest that useful data on extent of implementation can be collected by methods other than on-site observation.

Another possible approach to assess the extent of implementation is first to measure the number of program components delivered to target beneficiaries (perhaps to a sample of them) and then to estimate the percent of target recipients served. The overall degree of implementation is estimated by multiplying these two aspects: accuracy and scope. In sum, when program theory is such that an ideal program description can be specified in advance, the evaluator should use such specification to design measures of the extent of implementation, a key element of the evaluation plan.

When the program theory underlying the program is ambiguous or different theories are advanced by various stakeholders, usually the components of the program cannot be exactly specified in advance. In this case, the evaluator's role is to observe and record how and by whom the intervention is actually used in each study site. For example, in a recent study of office automation (Johnson and Associates, 1985) there was no single correct type of computer equipment, user configuration, nor types of office functions to be automated. Thus, it would not have been possible to design an evaluation instrument in advance to measure the extent and types of correct use. Instead, the researchers started with some general questions around this topic and then iteratively constructed a typology of office automation found to be related to other characteristics of the organizations being studied.

In such cases the data collection concerning extent of implementation may have to be iterative, with open-ended methods used initially to define the types of users and the functions performed. The program theories held by various participants can be tapped to suggest the range of activities that may be relevant. Such qualitative information is valuable in itself and can also be used to construct an instrument for larger scale, quantitative data collection. If program theory is not unified, the instrument should contain relevant measures of the various potential components related extent of implementation suggested by the program theories. The absence of a single unified theory can become the opportunity for comparative tests of multiple theories.

*Summary.* This discussion of the relationships between program theory and the measurement of the extent of program implementation is summarized in Table 1. As shown, the evaluator's roles are appropriately quite different, depending on whether the evaluation research is being done from a macro- or microperspective, or both. In each case, program theory should be the basis for specifying the program components that form the content for measuring extent of implementation. The types of data to collect in order to assess the extent of program implementation differ considerably, depending on the extent of prior program specification as well as perspective. Further, theories that should be used to develop the program design, and thus the evaluation design, also stem from quite different research traditions. These roles all reemphasize the nature of program evaluation as an interdisciplinary field, which needs a wide variety of skills, theories, and research approaches.

**Implementation Process Theory**

The preceding section on program theory discusses considerations in assessing what the program is and what treatment was delivered. Such considerations should be a sine qua non in any program evaluation design, as has been pointed out in several critiques of the overemphasis on outcome analysis (Lipsey and others, 1985; Sechrest and Redner, 1979). Beyond the issues involved in assessing what program was delivered, however, are questions concerning why variations in treatment delivery occur. These are the issues addressed by implementation process theory and research.

**Table 1. Assessing the Extent of Program Implementation: Summary of Evaluator's Roles**

| | | *Measurement Needed* (Depends on Prior Specification of Intervention) | |
|---|---|---|---|
| | *Type of Theory Applicable* | *Intervention Characteristics (Well-Specified)* | *Intervention Characteristics (Open-Ended)* |
| Macro (federal perspective) | Inter-organizational theory, especially on linkages across bureaucratic levels. | Accounting type measurement against *a priori* standards | Trace chain of influences through levels |
| Micro (local perspective) | Content area theory, used to define components. | Measure number and quality of components delivered; to how many recipients. | Measure range of activities, users, and immediate outcomes surrounding intervention. |

As evaluators find that variations in the extent of treatment delivery are associated with large differences in program effects, the next relevant questions for both evaluators and program administrators are likely to be why variations in treatment delivery occur and, more important, what can be done to improve delivery. Such issues can be easily studied empirically and are likely to become increasingly emphasized by evaluators. Such studies particularly draw from the extensive literature on organizational administration and change. For studies of implementation processes, the measures of extent or accuracy of implementation become the dependent variables. Measures of organizational characteristics and processes, program deliverers' backgrounds and activities, and other characteristics of the program itself become the independent or predictor variables in such studies.

Methodology for implementation process studies is not a single, standardized research paradigm. Some investigations have used qualitative methods, particularly case studies, to explore the links between the extent or types of program delivery and possible causal processes facilitating or hampering that extent (Pressman and Wildavsky, 1973; Ellickson and Petersilia, 1983). Other studies have estimated the strength of these relationships across several organizations using quantitative methods, particularly causal modeling of the social systems involved (Beyer and Trice, 1978) or a combination of methods (Smith and Louis, 1982). Further, the studies differ considerably in approach: Some use a macrolevel, program-administration-as-organizational-linkage perspective while others undertake a microlevel examination of variables relating to the extent of implementation within a specified set of organizations. Yet both types of methodology and both theoretical perspectives are valuable tools for evaluators to be aware of as potential contributions to evaluation designs.

Implementation process theory is much too broad an area to be fully discussed here. Further, its major branches are not yet well enough articulated even to be clearly distinguishable as theoretical approaches. Systematic reviews have been published by a group of researchers at the National Science Foundation (Tornatzky and others, 1983), as well as in my previous analysis of the organizational context of program implementation (Scheirer, 1981). Insightful contributions are provided by the literature on a number of organizational topics: organizational change, training and development, organizational life cycles, organization-environment relationships, and the diffusion of innovations into organizations, among others. However, even given the diversity of approaches, most implementation analysts seem to agree that a theoretical perspective drawing on the open social systems tradition is needed for research on this topic.

*Social Systems Perspective.* Perhaps the central assumption of a social systems approach to issues of implementation is that no single cause, no simple set of prescriptions, is likely to be found as *the* solution to these issues. The extent of implementation occurring for a particular program, within a specific organizational entity, is likely to be the result of the interrelationships among a number of elements in its encompassing social system. A major hypothesis is that the extent of implementation is likely to be higher when there is greater degree of congruence between the nature of the program or innovation being attempted and the characteristics of the organizational environments involved.

One implication of a social systems perspective is that a critical impediment to implementation can derive from a number of system elements. In essence, in program implementation there are many ways to fail. Consequently, obtaining adequate levels of implementation requires close attention to a wide range of system elements to ensure that each critical component is at least adequately favorable. The careful orchestration of people, resources, organizational processes, and program characteristics implies that the management of implementation should not be left to chance. A specific person or organizational component should have an explicit mandate, and sufficient resources, to oversee and manage the change process.

*Social System Components.* An overview of social system elements that are likely to be contributors to the extent of implementation can be summarized by discussing six types of components.

- The program or innovation itself
- Client inputs to the program
- Characteristics of the program deliverers
- Operating aspects of work units, such as normal routines, supervisory expectations, and communication channels
- The organizational structure for providing resources, making decisions, regulating the work flow, and so on
- Pressures from the organization's external environment.

An evaluator charged with assessing why a program intervention experienced differential extent of implementation in different sites should draw data from each of these six system components. By examining both the immediate program delivery and also the organizational features surrounding that delivery, the evaluator is more likely to understand the features within that social system that are producing and/or maintaining a given extent of program delivery. As the six components listed above suggest, such analysis is most illuminating when it encompasses multiple levels of organizational functioning, from variables characterizing the behavior of the front-line program deliverers, through aspects of their immediate work unit, to consideration of their organization as a whole, including the changing nature of its environment.

*The Program Itself.* A major aspect to be included in an implementation process analysis is the nature of the programs or innovations being implemented, particularly how fully they are specified in advance. For an intervention that has been fully developed, and preferably experimentally tested, the implementation task is to achieve faithful replication of its components in each adoption site. Implementation process study objectives are to uncover reasons for variability in the extent and accuracy of implementation. For interventions whose characteristics are not well specified in advance, a major research task is usually to describe actual variations in use, then to connect these variations with either causes or consequences.

This distinction between prespecified and to-be-developed program components is likely to resolve the apparent controversy over program adaptation versus program fidelity as an objective for implementation. Several analysts advocate an implementation process in which the innovation is freely adapted to fit the environment. Yet, these researchers have studied programs or innovations that were not (and in some cases, could not be) well specified in advance (Berman and McLaughlin, 1978; Yin, 1982; Eveland, Rogers, and Klepper, 1977). Other analysts who advocate implementation processes in which the innovation is reproduced with fidelity in each new site have usually studied innovations whose specific components have been developed and tested for effectiveness before the dissemination to new sites (see Blakely and others, 1984; Tornatzky and others, 1980). Thus, this rather heated controversy about appropriate implementation strategies can be resolved by differentiating different types of programs.

*Clients as Inputs to Program Processing.* For many social programs, a supply of clients is necessary, as the inputs to be changed by the program or other innovation (resources as inputs are discussed below). When planning or analyzing the implementation processes, the intended qualities of the clients as inputs to the program should be considered. For example, do job trainees have an adequate basic educational background to understand the specific training to be provided? Are the clients willing to participate if the program is voluntary? Are they available in sufficient numbers at the program location or will transportation be needed? If long-term follow-up is needed, how can high rates of client attrition be prevented? Although such details may seem to be routine administrative matters, the failure of these client inputs to match assumptions of program theory can lead to major implementation barriers.

*Characteristics of Program Deliverers.* Much has been written about the roles of the staff members participating in a new program, particularly their alleged resistance to change. The activities of the front-line deliverers are undoubtedly critical for achieving full implementation. These behaviors are likely to be influenced by many variables, particularly the extent of training (and sometimes educational background); staff members' incentives for achieving the change; and deliverers' underlying values, attitudes, and motivations as expressed in their jobs. (For a review of relevant literature, see Scheirer, 1981.) Individual differences among staff members are also likely to be reflected in differential extent of implementation. For example, front-line workers may hold various and perhaps outdated theories of how the program should work; these may differ from the theoretical intent of program developers and managers.

Yet, the social systems perspective suggests that the reactions of individuals to change are frequently based on workers' ongoing job frustrations or to their legitimate concerns about the relationships of the innovation to their own job roles or future advancement. Front-line workers are accustomed to higher authorities advocating unrealistic new programs only to see these programs quickly dropped when political administrations or program priorities change. Further, new programs are frequently promulgated without giving front-line workers the time, training, and supplies needed to support adequate implementation (see Weatherley and Lipsky, 1977). Some foot dragging is understandable by staff who have good reason to believe from past experience that the new program may not meet the needs of clients, will not be supported with necessary resources, or will be changed again before new work routines can be established that incorporate the intervention.

The scarcity of past attention to implementation processes in evaluation research is evident in the lack of implementation planning in program management. What systematic study is available indicates that there are substantial costs in the change-over process, which frequently are borne by front-line workers rather than by the organization. First, there is the time expended learning new procedures, new technology, and new ways of relating to other staff members. New procedures will likely take more time than old procedures, even if the program or technology is intended to increase efficiency. If front-line workers are expected to perform all their old duties plus learn the new program without being given time or additional assistance, they are likely to be substantially overloaded. Even under favorable organizational circumstances, the change-over period can require several months and can create a long period of job stress for staff members.

Also most workers have substantial human capital investments of training, seniority, and on-the-job experience that they may perceive as specific to the old technology or program. An innovation brought in from outside may seem to imply that those workers were not doing their jobs properly or make their human capital investments obsolete. The feared loss of the value of their expertise may result in real monetary losses for many workers; at the least, the devaluing of such expertise has an emotional cost for the worker. Without attention by management to the job pressures and potential losses faced by front-line workers, many program deliverers may develop cynical attitudes that can be viewed as a resistance to change.

*Operating Aspects of Work Units.* These situations faced by front-line workers suggests that their reactions to a new program are shaped by their immediate work environments; this is another premise of a social systems perspective. Organizations operate efficiently by establishing routines, or standard operating procedures, to guide workers' actions in different circumstances. A new program will be most compatible, and thus more easily implemented, when it fits within the established ways of doing things. The greater the need to change existing routines and roles, the greater the difficulty and time required to obtain full implementation, and the greater the change-over costs. For example, studies of medical interventions have shown that new types of drugs fit easily within the current structure of private practice medicine and thus are relatively readily adopted but that new types of health-related staff (for example, nurse practitioners or midwives) are less easily assimilated into the same organizational systems because changes in a number of established roles and routines are required (Greer, 1977; McKinlay, 1981).

The interrelationships of various workers' roles within a work unit can be critically important to program implementation. The supervisor's support for the program is most likely to be transmitted to workers. Even if the supervisors are not supposed to be in charge of the new program, their subordinates will look to them for guidance on organizational priorities and for approval of their work. Therefore, unit supervisors must be trained to understand the intervention and its underlying theory as well as how to reinforce their subordinates' efforts. Further, each work unit will likely have developed a set of informal norms (standards of behavior) about how the work will be done, how to interact with clients, and so forth. Such norms may or may not be supportive of the new program. Individual workers will also have evolved their own either informal or recognized role specializations that may be modified in content or usefulness by the innovation. Thus, several aspects of the ongoing role relationships within a work group are likely to affect and to be affected by the innovation. The ability of an implementation manager to diagnose and resolve conflicts in working relationships is likely to help make the transition period smoother. Similarly, diagnosing how role relationships are changed by a new program should be a key aspect of an implementation process study.

*Overall Organizational Structures.* A final organization level to consider in examining implementation support is the organization as a whole. The organization can support the implementation by facilitating decisions, providing necessary resources, setting organizational rules that support the innovation, and resolving competing priorities. A key initial predictor of implementation problems lies in how decisions are made about adopting the new program. A number of studies have found that without top-level backing and operational-level participation in such decision processes, a major innovation is unlikely to survive the implementation hurdles (Johnson and Associates, 1985; Louis and Rosenblum, 1981).

Yet, it is also highly desirable to have a specific person who champions the innovation from a position of seniority inside the organization (Bardach, 1977). Further, to the extent that the new program requires decision-making processes that are not congruent with the organization's usual procedures (such as collaborative planning in a hierarchically structured organization), implementation is also likely to be hampered.

Operating resources are another major component of any implementation process and are usually supplied from organizational-level resource allocation processes. Resource needs are frequently more than the immediate equipment and supplies used by the program. Implementation planners should consider at least the following categories of resources:

- Hardware, equipment, furniture
- Adequate staff with appropriate backgrounds, education, and innovation-specific training
- Information resources, such as computer software, program expertise, data about potential clients, and computer time
- Consumable supplies
- Maintenance and repair personnel for maintaining equipment
- Space for offices, meeting rooms, equipment, and so forth
- Program managers with sufficient time and authority to troubleshoot during the program's initial stages
- Adequate time to put together the program components without undue performance pressure.

Since time and resources estimates are frequently overly optimistic guesses concerning what will actually be needed, implementation plans should ideally include some slack resources to cover unforeseen contingencies.

*Environmental Pressures.* Finally, the implementation analyst should be aware of other environmental forces impinging on the organization that may create instabilities for the target program and for the implementing staff. Are funding sources derived from politically volatile external agencies or unpredictable sales markets? Are there regulating agencies that may constrain the intended program, specify the types of staff available to run it (such as the criteria used in the government employee rating systems), and create agency pressures for meeting competing priorities? Are there competitors for the participation of intended clients or staff? What is the overall community climate of support and interest for programmatic changes of the type envisioned? A wide range of such environmental pressures exists which constitutes additional potential hazards for the implementation process. Although it is not feasible to collect fully systematic data collection on all environmental variables, implementation managers and process evaluators should be alert to these potential influences.

Examining environmental pressures becomes a central concern, however, when the program is examined from the macroimplementation perspective. In this case, the operational links between program levels are the major focus; the analysis should examine the conflict or congruence between the linked organizations' missions, constituencies, available resources, and the intended program. For example, federal, state, and local level staff are likely to differ in the relative priority they place on equity of service delivery, maximizing revenues, maintaining a working political coalition, or other considerations that are affected by the new program. The extensive work on macroimplementation theory cited above provides a number of illuminating ideas about why interorganizational linkage is so cumbersome.

*Summary.* This section has provided a condensed overview of implementation process theory as an outline of the types of variables likely to influence the extent of program implementation, particularly at the micro/level of actual delivery. It has drawn from the social systems perspective to suggest the wide variety of individual and organizational processes that are likely to be affected by any major programmatic change. Knowledge of such processes is essential so that implementation managers can realistically plan for the difficulties their intended changes may create and so that implementation process evaluators can include the full range of relevant variables in their research designs.

Given the extensive scope of potentially influential variables, it is particularly desirable for implementation process studies to use multiple methods of data collection. In most moderately budgeted studies, it is unlikely that all the social system components can be measured with equal rigor. Yet, if several methods are used to monitor various potential trouble sources and the research design is kept flexible enough to increase the extent of data collection about unexpected hurdles, an implementation process evaluation should be useful to aid both program administrators and to increase long-term knowledge about these processes.

### Conclusions

This chapter has explored some relationships between program evaluation and two types of theory: program theory and implementation process theory. Although the two types of theory have developed from different disciplinary backgrounds, they are similar in their relationship to the central concept of the extent of implementation. Program theory suggests the program components that should be measured to describe the extent of implementation—the what of program delivery. Implementation process theory suggests the social system components that should be examined to explain and manage the extent of implementation—the how and why of program delivery.

From this perspective, evaluators' activities are much broader than focusing primarily on analyzing program outcomes. To understand program effects if they occur, the nature of the treatment must be described and the extent of its delivery measured. For this task, the evaluator should become familiar with relevant program theory. To monitor the reasons underlying variations in the extent of program delivery and to provide timely feedback to correct inadequate delivery, program evaluators should include implementation process theory in their repertoires. From this expanded selection of potential evaluation designs, program managers and evaluators can choose the research designs and appropriate data collection and analysis strategies that best fit the particular situation.

## References

Bardach, E. *The Implementation Game: What Happens After a Bill Becomes a Law.* Cambridge, Mass.: MIT Press, 1977.

Berman, P. "The Study of Macro- and Micro-Implementation." *Public Policy,* 1978, *26* (2), 157–184.

Berman, P., and McLaughlin, M. W. *Federal Programs Supporting Educational Change.* Vol. 8. *Implementing and Sustaining Innovations.* A report prepared for the U.S. Office of Education. Santa Monica, Calif.: Rand Corporation, 1978.

Beyer, J. M., and Trice, H. M. *Implementing Change: Alcoholism Policies in Work Organizations.* New York: Free Press, 1978.

Blakely, C., Mayer, J., Gottschalk, R., Roitman, D., Schmitt, N., Davidson II, W., and Emshoff, J. *Salient Processes in the Dissemination of Social Technologies.* Final Report submitted to the National Science Foundation of Grant No. ISI 7920576-01. East Lansing: Michigan State University, 1984.

Bryk, A. S. (ed.). *Stakeholder-Based Evaluation.* New Directions for Program Evaluation, no. 17. San Francisco: Jossey-Bass, 1983.

Chelimsky, E. "Comparing and Contrasting Auditing and Evaluation: Some Notes on Their Relationship." *Evaluation Review,* 1985, *9* (4), 483–503.

Colton, R. M. "National Science Foundation Experience with University-Industry Center for Scientific Research and Technological Innovation: An Analysis of Issues, Characteristics, and Criteria for Their Establishment." *Technovation,* 1981, *1,* 97–108.

Ellickson, P., and Petersilia, J. *Implementing New Ideas in Criminal Justice.* Report prepared for the National Institute of Justice, U.S. Dept. of Justice. Santa Monica, Calif.: Rand Corporation, 1983.

Elmore, R. F. "Backward Mapping: Implementation Research and Policy Decisions." In W. Williams and others (eds.), *Studying Implementation: Methodological and Administrative Issues.* Chatham: N.J.: Chatham House, 1982.

Eveland, J. D., Rogers, E. M., and Klepper, C. A. *The Innovation Process in Public Organizations: Some Elements of a Preliminary Model.* Final report to the National Science Foundation, Grant No. RDA-7517952. Ann Arbor: University of Michigan, 1977.

Greer, A. L. "Advances in the Study of Diffusion of Innovation in Health Care Organizations." *Milbank Memorial Fund Quarterly: Health and Society,* 1977, *55,* 505–532.

Johnson, B. M., and Associates. *Innovation in Office Systems Implementation.* National Science Foundation Report. No. 8110791. Norman: Department of Communication, University of Oklahoma, 1985.

Lipsey, M. W., Crosse, S., Dunkle, J., Pollard, J., and Stobart, G. "Evaluation: The State of the Art and the Sorry State of the Science." In D. S. Cordray (ed.), *Utilizing Prior Research in Evaluation Planning.* New Directions for Program Evaluation, no. 27. San Francisco: Jossey-Bass, 1985.

76

Louis, K. S., and Rosenblum, S. *Linking R & D with Schools: A Program and Its Implications for Dissemination and School Improvement Policy.* Washington, D.C.: U.S. Department of Education, National Institute of Education, 1981.

McKinlay, J. B. "From 'Promising Report' to 'Standard Procedure': Seven Stages in the Career of a Medical Innovation." *Milbank Memorial Fund Quarterly/ Health and Society,* 1981, *59,* 374–411.

Mark, M. M., and Shotland, R. L. "Stakeholder-Based Evaluation and Value Judgments." *Evaluation Review,* 1985, *9* (5), 605–626.

Pressman, J. L., and Wildavsky, A. B. *Implementation.* Berkeley: University of California Press, 1973.

Sabatier, P., and Mazmanian, D. "The Conditions of Effective Implementation: A Guide to Accomplishing Policy Objectives." *Policy Analysis,* 1979, *5,* 481–504.

Scheirer, M. A. *Program Implementation: The Organizational Context.* Beverly Hills, Calif.: Sage, 1981.

Scheirer, M. A., Nieva, V. F., Gaertner, G. H., Newman, P. D., and Ramsey, V. F. *Innovation and Enterprise: A Study of NSF's Innovation Centers Program.* Rockville, Md.: Westat, 1985.

Sechrest, L., and Redner, R. "Strength and Integrity of Treatments in Evaluation Studies." In *How Well Does It Work? Review of Criminal Justice Evaluation, 1978.* Washington, D.C.: U.S. National Criminal Justice Reference Service, Department of Justice, 1979.

Smith, A. G., and Louis, K. S. (eds.). "Multimethod Policy Research: Issues and Applications." *American Behavioral Scientist,* 1982, *26* (1), entire issue.

Tornatzky, L. G., Eveland, J. D., Boylan, M. G., Hetzner, W. A., Johnson, E. C., Roitman, D., and Schneider, J. *The Process of Technological Innovation: Reviewing the Literature.* Washington, D.C.: National Science Foundation, 1983.

Tornatzky, L. G., Fergus, E. O., Avellar, J. W., Fairweather, G. W., and Fleischer, M. *Innovation and Social Process: A National Experiment in Implementing Social Technology.* Elmsford, N.Y.: Pergamon, 1980.

Weatherley, R., and Lipsky, M. "Street-Level Bureaucrats and Institutional Innovation: Implementing Special Education Reform." *Harvard Educational Review,* 1977, *47,* 171–197.

Williams, W. *The Implementation Perspective.* Berkeley: University of California Press, 1980.

Yin, R. "Studying the Implementation of Public Programs." In W. Williams and others (eds.), *Studying Implementation: Methodological and Administrative Issues.* Chatham, N.J.: Chatham House, 1982.

Yin, R. K., Quick, S. K., Bateman, P. M. and Marks, E. L. *Changing Urban Bureaucracies: How New Practices Become Routinized.* Lexington, Mass.: Heath, 1979.

*Mary Ann Scheirer is senior behavioral scientist with Westat, Inc., Rockville, Maryland. She is a social psychologist who applies social systems analysis to research on the implementation of organizational, technical, and social changes. Her earlier work on the implementation of innovations was published as* Program Implementation: The Organizational Context *(1981).*

*Evaluability assessment involves key policymakers, managers, and staff in developing program theory and clarifying intended uses of evaluation information, thus helping solve problems that inhibit useful program evaluation.*

# Evaluability Assessment: Developing Program Theory

*Joseph S. Wholey*

Program evaluation includes the measurement of program performance (resource expenditures, program activities, and program outcomes) and the testing of causal assumptions linking program resources, activities, and outcomes. One important potential use of program evaluation is its use by key policymakers, managers, and staff to change program activities or objectives in ways that will lead to improved program performance: greater efficiency, greater effectiveness, or greater net benefits. Horst, Nay, Scanlon, and Wholey (1974) and Wholey (1983a) identify four problems that inhibit such uses of evaluation.

1. Lack of definition of the problem addressed, the program intervention, the expected outcomes of the program, or the expected impact on the problem addressed.

2. Lack of a clear logic of testable assumptions linking expenditure of program resources, the implementation of the program, the outcomes to be caused by that program, and the resulting impact.

Leonard Bickman suggested the topic for this chapter and provided helpful advice as it took shape. Christopher Bellavita, Cynthia McSwain, Beryl Radin, Debra Rog, Ronald Stupak, Margaret Wholey, and an anonymous reviewer provided very helpful comments on the manuscript.

L. Bickman (ed.). *Using Program Theory in Evaluation.*
New Directions for Program Evaluation, no. 33. San Francisco: Jossey-Bass, Spring 1987.

3. Lack of agreement on evaluation priorities and intended uses of evaluation.

4. Inability or unwillingness to act on the basis of evaluation information.

If any of the first three problems exists, evaluation often proves to be inconclusive or irrelevant. If the third or fourth problem exists, even relevant, conclusive evaluations are unlikely to produce improvements in program performance.

Evaluability assessment is a diagnostic and prescriptive tool that can be used to determine the extent to which any of these four problems exists and to help ensure that such problems are solved before decisions are made to proceed with any further evaluation. Evaluability assessment clarifies program intent from the points of view of key actors in and around the program; explores program reality to clarify the plausibility of program objectives and the feasibility of performance measurements; and identifies opportunities to change program resources, activities, objectives, and uses of information in ways likely to improve program performance. Evaluability assessment is typically done as part of the planning and design of evaluations or the development of management information systems or outcome monitoring systems. Although evaluability assessment (as its name implies) explores the feasibility of program evaluations, another important focus of evaluability assessment is the likely usefulness of evaluation in improving program performance.

The evaluability assessment process is described in Schmidt, Scanlon, and Bell (1979), Wholey (1979), Rutman (1980), Nay and Kay (1982), and Wholey (1983a). Rog (1985) examines the uses of fifty-seven evaluability assessments conducted by the Department of Health and Human Services and the Department of Education from 1972 to 1984. This chapter examines relationships between evaluability assessment and program theory, illustrates key issues with examples from a state health department and a large nonprofit organization, and discusses the significance of evaluability assessment and program theory in evaluation planning.

**Developing Program Theory: Clarifying Intended Uses of Evaluation**

A program is a set of resources and activities directed toward one or more common goals, typically under the direction of a single manager or a management team. A program theory identifies program resources, program activities, and intended program outcomes, and specifies a chain of causal assumptions linking program resources, activities, intermediate outcomes, and ultimate goals. Like the examples presented below, program theories can be expressed in the following form: *"If* the following program resources are available, *then* the following program activities will be undertaken. . . . *If* these program activities occur, *then* the following program outcomes will be produced. . . . *If* these activities and outcomes occur, *then* progress will be made toward the following program goals." Evaluability assessment involves key policymakers, managers, and staff in developing and clarifying program theories, testing and refining program theories, deciding on changes in program activities or objectives that appear likely to improve program performance, and deciding on evaluation priorities and intended uses of evaluation information.

*Involving Key Policymakers, Managers, and Staff.* Contrary to the many evaluation planning efforts in which evaluators operate in virtual isolation from policymakers and program staff, evaluability assessment encourages a series of interactions between evaluators and key policymakers, managers, and staff. These interactions are designed to ensure that the program theory developed by the evaluators conforms to the expectations of those who have the greatest influence over and involvement in the program. Evaluability assessment also helps shape those expectations by informing key policymakers and managers of the expectations of others, by confronting policymakers and managers with the reality of the program as it is currently operating, and by helping policymakers and managers explore the implications of possible changes in program activities or objectives.

In evaluability assessment, key policymakers, managers, and staff are drawn into continuing involvement in evaluation activities. They provide information, react to tentative descriptive and explanatory models, make program changes to enhance program performance, and focus further evaluation efforts on the collection and analysis of information that is likely to be used to improve program performance.

In recent years, many evaluability assessments have used policy groups and work groups to facilitate policymaker, manager, and staff involvement in evaluation planning. Work groups involve key program staff in evaluability assessment activities on an ongoing basis (Rog, 1985). Policy groups involve higher-level managers and policymakers, who are briefed periodically on findings and options as the evaluability assessment proceeds (Wholey, 1983a).

*Developing and Clarifying Program Theory.* Much evaluation work has been criticized as atheoretic. Other evaluation work is theory based but is either disconnected from important aspects of program reality or irrelevant to the information needs of those who have the power to bring about program change. In the absence of clear theory that is grounded both in program reality and in the expectations of those who have the greatest influence over the program, it is difficult to design evaluations that will be sufficiently relevant and conclusive to be used to improve program performance.

For many programs, however, the underlying theory is vague or is missing entirely. Too much precision about intended program activities or objectives might have inhibited the political compromises needed to initiate the program or to gain the resources needed for program maintenance or expansion. In many problem areas, moreover, insufficient knowledge is available to specify the types of program activities or outcomes that are likely to contribute to progress toward program goals.

Thus, an important part of the evaluability assessment process is the construction of models that clarify the assumed relationships among program resources, program activities, and expected outcomes from the points of view of key policymakers, managers, and interest groups. In constructing these models, evaluators get clues about the theories underlying the program both from relevant documents and from a series of interactions with those who have the greatest influence over the program. Relevant documentation on program intent may include the program's legislative history, regulations and guidelines, budget justifications, monitoring reports, and reports of accomplishments. The evaluators pinpoint current expectations and indications of problem areas from interviews with several policymakers, managers, and interest group representatives, as well as from the site visits discussed below. These interviews focus on program priorities, expected program accomplishments, relationships between objectives and the resources that would be needed to achieve the objectives, difficulties facing the program, and information needs.

In subsequent meetings with program managers and policymakers, the evaluators use models of program resources, activities, and intended outcomes to highlight differences in expectations and to facilitate agreement on the intended program: program resources, activities, intended outcomes, important potential side effects, and assumed causal linkages among resources, activities, and outcomes. These meetings ensure that the evaluators have accurately captured program theory as understood by those who have the greatest influence over the program and ensure that discrepancies over resources, activities, objectives, and causal assumptions are understood and, if possible, resolved. In the meetings, current and possible new measures of program resources, activities, and outcomes are also reviewed to ensure that there is a common understanding of concepts and variables to be used in subsequent evaluation activities.

*Testing and Refining Program Theory.* To test and refine the program models developed in the first phase of evaluability assessment, the evaluators use available documents, site visits, and another series of interactions with those in charge of the program. The evaluators use relevant documents on program reality (monitoring reports, reports of program accomplishments, audit reports, and research and evaluation studies) and a small number of site visits to compare the intended program with actual program activities and outcomes; to make estimates of the likelihood of effective program performance in terms of the concepts, variables, and assumptions identified in the initial program models; and to identify changes in program activities or objectives that might be made to improve program performance. The site visits provide information on the extent to which the intended program has been implemented, on local goals and objectives, on obstacles to effective program performance, and on important side effects of program activities. The documents and site visits also provide information on feasible measures of concepts and variables in the program models.

When the initial program models are compared with program reality, it is often clear that program theories need adjustment. In some cases, program objectives are implausible, or needed program performance information cannot be obtained within reasonable cost constraints. In other cases (for example, in programs that permit a great deal of local autonomy), higher-level managers and policymakers may find that the program's actual accomplishments suggest the desirability of adopting additional program objectives that capture some of those accomplishments.

In one or more meetings, the evaluators brief key managers and policymakers on (1) what has been learned about program performance and performance problems, (2) the implications of continuing to operate the program as it is currently being operated, (3) changes in program activities or objectives that could lead to improved program performance, (4) the implications of potential program changes in terms of resource requirements and implementation issues, (5) evaluation information that could be collected, and (6) the cost implications of evaluation options. Decisions to change the program would imply revisions in program theory. Decisions to proceed with additional evaluation efforts would focus evaluation resources on specific portions of the intended program: measuring specific variables of interest to policymakers or managers, or testing specific causal assumptions that appear in the program model.

*Clarifying Intended Uses of Evaluation Information.* To avoid the problem of information in search of a user, evaluability assessments often offer evaluation options as management options, which specify the primary intended uses of any additional evaluation information. When policymakers or managers select such evaluation options, they are at least tentatively agreeing on how the resulting information would be used. By exploring the implications of no further evaluation as well as the potential uses of additional evaluation, the evaluator encourages policymakers and managers to commit themselves to intended uses of evaluation information when decisions are made to collect and analyze any additional information on program performance.

### Tennessee's Prenatal Program

In the Tennessee Department of Public Health, evaluability assessment was used to clarify the theory underlying the department's prenatal care program and to determine which evaluation activities would be most useful as federal project grant funding came to an end. (Wholey [1983a] and Smith [1986] discuss this evaluability assessment and its results.)

In July 1981 the Tennessee Department of Public Health began the last year of a five-year federally funded $400,000 per year project, "Toward Improving the Outcome of Pregnancy." This project provided funds for prenatal care of low-income patients in seven regional projects that operated in nineteen rural health departments. The Department of Public Health faced reductions in federal funding and likely constraints on the availability of state funding for prenatal care. An evaluation of the nineteen-county demonstration program was initiated, as had been contemplated under the terms of the federal grant.

***Evaluability Assessment Process and Products.*** As had been proposed in the evaluation consultants' response to the department's request for proposals, the evaluators used evaluability assessment in producing the proposed design for evaluation of Tennessee's prenatal program. In a total of forty-eight staff days of effort over a five-week period in June and July 1981, two evaluation consultants worked with Department of Public Health staff to plan an evaluation of the prenatal program and to establish a decision process that would use the evaluation findings. During this time, the evaluators held a series of working meetings with managers and staff, reviewed documents describing the project and related prenatal services, and visited one of the regional projects. These activities helped the evaluators (1) identify likely users of the planned evaluation; (2) clarify the theory underlying the prenatal program; (3) compare the intended prenatal program with actual program resources, activities, and outcomes; (4) determine the likely availability of relevant data; and (5) determine which of the feasible evaluation alternatives would be most relevant and useful.

To facilitate the evaluation and its use, the evaluators encouraged the department to establish a work group and a policy group that would provide ongoing input to the evaluation. The work group included key central office maternal and child health staff and staff from three of the regional prenatal projects. The policy group included management staff from region, section, and bureau levels; the deputy commissioner of public health; and key budget staff from the Department of Public Health and the Department of Finance and Administration.

The evaluators identified intended prenatal program resources, activities, outcomes, and assumed causal linkages through analyses of program documentation and notes from interviews and working meetings with managers and staff. Figure 1 presents the theory underlying Tennessee's prenatal program as that program was seen by Department of Public Health managers and staff. Through implementation of model projects in selected high-risk areas across the state, Tennessee's prenatal program sought to bring together state, regional, and local agencies and private

# Figure 1. Tennessee's Prenatal Program

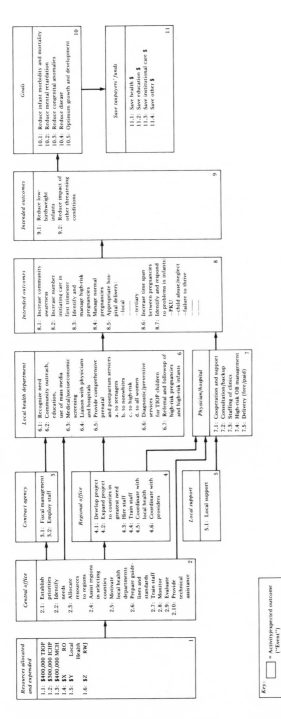

*Source:* Wholey and Wholey, 1981a, pp. 111-3a, 111-3b. Reprinted by permission of the publisher.

providers to develop comprehensive systems for the delivery of prenatal care to low-income patients. Central office staff were expected to provide planning, guidelines and standards, training, monitoring and evaluation, and technical assistance. Regional office staff were expected to assist in project development, hiring and training of staff, and coordination with local health departments and private providers. Local health departments were expected to provide community outreach, screening and diagnostic services, comprehensive prenatal services, and referral and follow-up of high-risk pregnancies and high-risk infants. Private providers were asked to provide cooperation and support, including consultation and back up, staffing of clinics, management of high-risk cases, and delivery (with or without partial payment from project budgets). It was expected that the program would (1) increase the numbers of low-income women entering prenatal care in their first trimester of pregnancy; (2) reduce the numbers of low-birthweight infants (infants with birthweight less than 5.5 pounds); and (3) reduce infant morbidity, mortality, and mental retardation. Figure 1 presents the theory underlying Tennessee's prenatal care program in a program design model that facilitated agreement among policymakers, managers, and staff on the intended program and on priorities for the planned evaluation.

On the basis of interviews with Department of Public Health staff, annual reports from regional health offices and prenatal projects, project budgets and expenditure reports, data from the prenatal program's quarterly reporting system, monitoring reports by central office staff, and a site visit to one of the regional projects, the evaluators determined that Tennessee's actual prenatal program closely resembled the intended program but had a number of problems that could threaten effective performance. On the basis of the information available, the evaluators concluded that none of the program objectives appeared implausible. No changes in program activities or objectives were suggested at this time.

*Results.* The evaluability assessment resulted in (1) agreement among evaluators and key policymakers, managers, and staff on the theory underlying Tennessee's prenatal care program (intended program inputs, activities, and outcomes, and assumed causal linkages among intended inputs, activities, and outcomes); and (2) agreement on the objectives that would be the major focus of the evaluation. The evaluation would focus particular attention on whether the prenatal care program was effective in reducing numbers of low-birthweight infants: Low birthweight is known to be closely associated with infant morbidity and mortality and with mental retardation; reduction of the incidence of low birthweight was an outcome objective that program managers considered realistic.

After review of information on the intended program and the actual program, the department agreed to focus the evaluation on a subset of the intended program that included resources expended, numbers of patients served, types of services delivered, trimester in which prenatal care was initiated, and incidence of low birthweight. It was agreed that the evaluation would be used in budget decisions for fiscal year 1983, in planning for the prenatal care to be provided in fiscal year 1983 and beyond, in developing formulas for allocation of funds to maintain or expand prenatal services, in reexamination of the guidelines and standards for prenatal care, and in regional and local decisions on the types of prenatal care to be provided. Although the evaluation contract had included a planned evaluation of the prenatal program in terms of the input and process objectives stated in the original grant application, it was agreed that the evaluation would *not* focus on those objectives, since the annual project reports to the federal government had monitored progress in terms of those objectives and interviews with Department of Public Health staff and had revealed relatively little demand for additional information on progress toward those objectives.

The evaluability assessment resulted in the decision to add to the evaluation an interim report that would be available by November 1981, for use in the state's budget process for fiscal year 1983. The interim evaluation (Wholey and Wholey, 1981b) found that the prenatal program had reduced the incidence of low birthweight: Information that the evaluators compiled from project reports and other available data indicated that the incidence of low birthweight among infants born to prenatal program patients was well below the incidence of low birthweight in appropriate comparison groups.

Smith (1986) notes the interim evaluation was used in preparation of the department's plan to expand prenatal care throughout Tennessee and was used in the budget deliberations over the proposed statewide program. The interim evaluation was also used in establishing plausible objectives for improved prenatal care throughout Tennessee: securing the cooperation of private physicians; maximizing Medicaid reimbursement to local health departments for prenatal care; early initiation of prenatal care; and reduction of the incidence of low birthweight, neonatal mortality, and infant mortality.

Although the politically powerful Governor's Task Force on Mental Retardation had already called for improvements in prenatal care, it appears that the interim evaluation was also a factor in the executive branch decision to propose $2 million in state appropriations for the initiation of a statewide prenatal program at what otherwise was a time of budget retrenchment in Tennessee. The positive evaluation findings were used in advocacy within the executive branch for inclusion of the $2 million request in the governor's fiscal year 1983 budget. The evaluation helped keep this budget issue alive when it appeared that the governor's budget would propose only a $500,000 appropriation to continue the pilot projects.

### Aid Association for Lutherans' Fraternal Benefit Programs

At Aid Association for Lutherans (AAL), evaluability assessment was applied to a group of forty programs, which were treated in the analysis as if they were one program. Here the purpose was not the evaluation of a single program. Instead, the intent was to develop the theoretical base for an effort to improve the management, performance, and credibility of a forty-program organizational unit. (Wholey [1983b] and Bickel [1986] discuss this evaluability assessment and its results.)

*Context.* AAL is a fraternal benefit society that provides life insurance and other services to approximately 1.3 million members. A tax-exempt organization, it also provides fraternal benefits to member families and other individuals and to Lutheran and community organizations: approximately $15 million per year in service, education, and charitable programs. In January 1983 AAL's fraternal operations department faced likely financial constraints. Although the department had committed substantial resources to evaluation of fraternal benefit programs, previous evaluations had not made significant contributions to decision making. Although the department's policies required that all programs be evaluated every five years, in practice only the largest programs were evaluated. These evaluations, which usually documented lack of agreement on program objectives and other weaknesses in program design, were not focused on policy, budget, or management decisions.

In preparation for decisions on the future of the fraternal benefit programs, AAL asked an evaluation consultant to undertake an evaluability assessment of the constellation of forty programs treated as one program. AAL staff had become familiar with evaluability assessment through a series of two-day training events that the consultant had conducted, using AAL programs as examples. Evaluability assessment of the forty-program fraternal benefit program was intended to achieve policy-level and management agreement on the most important objectives of AAL's fraternal benefit programs, the types of evidence that would indicate progress toward those objectives, and planned uses of evaluation to achieve and demonstrate effective performance.

*Evaluability Assessment Process and Products.* In a total of forty-six staff days of effort over an eight-month period from January through August 1983, the evaluation consultant (1) reviewed relevant documents; (2) interviewed fraternal operations department managers and staff, executives in the insurance operations department and at corporate level, and the president of AAL; (3) and met with the Fraternal and Benevolence Committee of the corporation's board of directors. These activities were designed to clarify the theory underlying the fraternal benefit programs and the extent of progress that was likely toward those objectives and to determine which evaluation alternatives would be feasible and useful.

Figure 2 presents the theory underlying the fraternal benefit programs as those programs were seen by AAL policymakers and managers. Resources for fraternal benefit programs included AAL members, home office and field staff, volunteers, information, and money. In 1983 AAL allocated approximately $15 million per year to fraternal benefit programs; local branches raised and contributed another $4 million per year under AAL's Co-op Benevolence Program. Directly and through the local branches, fraternal benefits were provided to AAL members and other Lutherans, to Lutheran congregations and organizations, and to individuals and groups in the local community. The fraternal benefit programs were expected (1) to achieve high participation rates among targeted recipients, (2) to meet real needs among recipients, (3) to contribute to enhanced awareness and approval among various internal and external constituencies (members, branch officers, field staff, corporate level, Lutheran church officials, legislators, and regulators), and (4) to strengthen AAL's local branches. Figure 2 is a revised version of a more complex program model that synthesized the expectations of the board's Fraternal and Benevolence Committee and AAL's president, insurance operations division and corporate-level executives, the head of the fraternal operations department and his executive staff, and the heads of the fraternal benefit development and fraternal benefit administration subdivisions. Despite differences in expectations that were made clear to the department, the evaluator concluded that there was a high degree of consistency in the expectations of AAL policymakers and managers.

The evaluability assessment documented three problems in AAL's fraternal benefit programs, as follows: (1) Resources were spread too thin to solve important problems, (2) the fraternal benefit programs faced resource constraints and pressures to reduce administrative costs, (3) valid, reliable information was lacking on the performance of most of the fraternal benefit programs.

In addition to an option that would have maintained the status quo, the evaluability assessment suggested three options for achieving and demonstrating effective performance in AAL's fraternal benefit programs, as follows: (1) manage to achieve optimal participation in (and satisfaction with) AAL's fraternal benefit programs, (2) manage to meet real needs among program recipients, (3) manage to meet real needs and to enhance recognition and approval of AAL programs. Under the last option, the fraternal operations department would concentrate the bulk of its fraternal benefit resources on meeting a manageable number of real needs among program recipients, adjust to resource constraints while building the best possible case for increased resources, and develop better performance measures and better systems for credibly assessing and communicating fraternal benefit program accomplishments. The evaluability assessment report (Wholey, 1983b) explored the cost, timing, and political and bureaucratic implications of each of the options.

# Figure 2. AAL's Fraternal Benefit Program

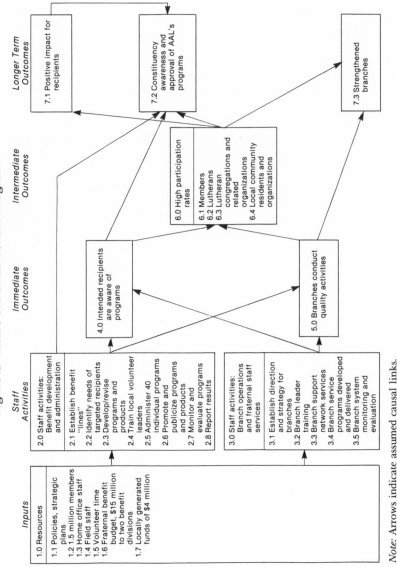

*Note:* Arrows indicate assumed causal links.

*Source:* Bickel, 1986, p. 23. Reprinted by permission of the publisher.

*Results.* In July and August 1983 the evaluator scheduled a series of telephone interviews with fraternal operations department managers and a series of meetings with fraternal operations department management committees and the Board's Fraternal and Benevolence Committee. The purposes of these interviews and meetings were to document reactions to the evaluability assessment findings and options and to facilitate decisions on management options and implementation steps. In the interviews and meetings, AAL policymakers, managers, and staff were asked to react to and suggest necessary revisions to an earlier version of the program design model (Figure 2) and to react to the problems, options, and implementation steps outlined in the evaluability assessment report. In the interviews and meetings, fraternal operations department managers agreed that they would concentrate resources on fewer fraternal benefit programs and agreed on four objectives as a framework for managing and evaluating the fraternal benefit programs, namely, high participation rates, meeting real needs of primary target groups, strengthening AAL's local branches, and enhancing awareness and approval among internal and external constituencies.

As a result of the evaluability assessment, the fraternal operations department decided to undertake a Results-Oriented Management initiative designed to improve the management and performance of existing and future fraternal benefit programs and to assist in credibly communicating program objectives and results to important internal and external constituencies. This initiative was pilot tested in late 1983 and then expanded to an effort that would evaluate and decide on the future of each of the forty fraternal benefit programs by the end of 1986. Within the framework of the four objectives for AAL's fraternal benefit program, the Results-Oriented Management initiative was designed to (1) get agreement on the expected outcomes of each of the forty programs and agreement on the types of evidence that would indicate whether those outcome objectives were being met; (2) use information on program outcomes in decisions to expand, modify, or phase out individual programs; and (3) use information on program outcomes in managing programs and in communicating objectives and results to important internal and external constituencies. The initiative established a framework in which information on program performance would be the most important factor in decisions as to whether to promote, modify, or phase out individual programs and established a process in which small-sample, rapid-feedback evaluations would be used as inputs to periodic decision conferences on portions of the fraternal benefit program portfolio.

Evaluability assessment of AAL's fraternal benefit programs clarified the theory underlying program activities and produced an agreed-on fraternal benefit program. The agreed-on program model facilitated evaluation and management of the forty-program fraternal benefit program portfolio as a single program. Fraternal operations department managers have since used information on the performance of the individual programs in decisions intended to improve the efficiency, effectiveness, and value of the fraternal benefit program. By December 1985

1. Twenty-nine of the forty fraternal benefit programs had been evaluated. (These programs accounted for approximately $12 million of the $16 million in benefit program costs in 1985.)

2. Decisions had been made to phase out eight of the twenty-nine programs. (These programs accounted for approximately $1.2 million of the $12 million in programs that had been evaluated.)

3. Decisions had been made to revise eleven of the other programs to improve program performance.

4. New fraternal benefit programs were being designed with clearer outcome objectives, many accompanied by agreed-on performance measures and target levels of intended performance.

## Significance

Useful program evaluation is inhibited by four problems, namely (1) lack of definition of the problem addressed and of the program itself, (2) lack of a clear logic of testable assumptions linking expenditure of resources to intended impacts, (3) lack of agreement on evaluation priorities, and (4) unwillingness to act on the basis of evaluation information. Through development and clarification of program theory, evaluability assessment facilitates solution of the first two of these problems. Evaluability assessment facilitates agreement among key managers and policymakers on realistic, measurable objectives and important potential side effects on the program and on a logic of testable assumptions linking program inputs, program activities, intermediate outcomes, and ultimate program impacts.

In evaluability assessment evaluators do not construct program theory by relying on their own knowledge and expertise. Instead, as in Tennessee's prenatal program and Aid Association for Lutherans' fraternal benefit program, evaluators involve key policymakers, managers, and staff in activities that develop, clarify, and refine the theory underlying the program to be evaluated, from the perspectives of those who have the greatest influence over the program. In evaluability assessment, the evaluator's approach to program theory is consistent with that of Glaser and Strauss (1967), who emphasize the researcher's use of conceptual categories and generalized relationships that emerge from data rather than the use of a priori categories and hypotheses. In evaluability assessment evaluators collect data on the expectations of key actors and on the reality of program operations as part of the evaluation planning process. When a program has been designed and operated on a clear theoretical base, evaluability assessment makes the theoretical base explicit before choices are made on measures, sample sizes, and tests of specific causal assumptions. When a program lacks such a theoretical base, evaluability assessment helps policymakers and managers supply that base as a first step in evaluation planning.

Evaluability assessment is most useful in large, decentralized programs in which policymaking and management responsibilities are dispersed and results are not readily apparent. Evaluability assessment helps key managers and staff understand, and in some cases modify, the expectations of those who have the most important influence over the program. By recognizing recurring patterns in interview notes, extracts from program documents, and site-visit reports, evaluators develop key concepts and variables that identify important intended program inputs, activities, intermediate outcomes, and longer-term outcomes—and thus take the first step in clarifying the theory underlying program activities. By identifying assumed causal linkages among program inputs, activities, and outcomes (from interview notes, program documents, site-visit reports, and knowledge of other similar programs), evaluators take the second step in developing program theory. Evaluators clarify differences among the assumptions and expectations of key policymakers, managers, and relevant interest groups—and document differences between intended and actual program inputs, activities, and outcomes. Subsequent meetings with managers and policymakers ensure that there is a common understanding of program theory before further evaluation work is undertaken. Evaluability assessment often develops policymaker-management consensus on program intent that is sufficiently strong to outlast changes of these key individuals.

Evaluability assessment helps policymakers and managers agree on key aspects of program theory that are to be tested in subsequent evaluations, namely, expected activities and outcomes that will be monitored and causal assumptions that will be tested. Thus, evaluability assessment helps solve the third problem inhibiting useful evaluation. As in Tennessee's prenatal program, evaluability assessment tends to focus evaluation resources on intermediate outcome objectives that are subject to the influence of, but not completely under the control of, managers.

Finally, evaluability assessment encourages policymakers and managers to act on the basis of evaluation information. As in Aid Association for Lutherans' fraternal benefit program, evaluability assessment is often useful in the planning of evaluations that will be used to stimulate improved program performance. On occasion, as in Tennessee's prenatal program, evaluability assessment can also be useful in planning evaluations that executives and managers will use to convince others of the value of the program.

## References

Bickel, K. L. "Organizing Evaluation to Improve the Performance of a Nonprofit Organization." In J. S. Wholey, M. A. Abramson, and C. Bellavita (eds.), *Perfor-*

*mance and Credibility: Developing Excellence in Public and Nonprofit Organizations.* Lexington, Mass.: Heath, 1986.

Glaser, B. G., and Strauss, A. L. *The Discovery of Grounded Theory. Strategies for Qualitative Research.* Hawthorne, N.Y.: Aldine, 1967.

Horst, P., Nay, J. N., Scanlon, J. W., and Wholey, J. S. "Program Management and the Federal Evaluator." *Public Administration Review,* 1974, *34,* 300–308.

Nay, J., and Kay, P. *Government Oversight and Evaluability Assessment.* Lexington, Mass.: Heath, 1982.

Rog, D. J. "A Methodological Analysis of Evaluability Assessment." Unpublished doctoral dissertation, Vanderbilt University, 1985.

Rutman, L. *Planning Useful Evaluations: Evaluability Assessment.* Beverly Hills, Calif.: Sage, 1980.

Schmidt, R. E., Scanlon, J. W., and Bell, J. B. *Evaluability Assessment: Making Public Programs Work Better.* Rockville, Md.: Project Share, Department of Health and Human Services, 1979.

Smith, J. D. "Communicating the Value of Tennessee's Prenatal Program." In J. S. Wholey, M. A. Abramson, and C. Bellavita (eds.), *Performance and Credibility: Developing Excellence in Public and Nonprofit Organizations.* Lexington, Mass.: Heath, 1986.

Wholey, J. S. *Evaluation: Promise and Performance.* Washington, D.C.: Urban Institute, 1979.

Wholey, J. S. *Evaluation and Effective Public Management.* Boston: Little, Brown, 1983a.

Wholey, J. S. *A Results-Oriented Approach to Managing AAL's Noninsurance Benefit Programs.* Arlington, Va.: Wholey Asociates, 1983b.

Wholey, J. S., and Wholey, M. S. *Evaluation of TIOP and Related Prenatal Care Programs: Proposed Approach to Parts A, B, and C of the Evaluation.* Report prepared for the Tennessee Department of Public Health. Arlington, Va.: Wholey Associates, 1981a.

Wholey, J. S., and Wholey, M. S. *Evaluation of TIOP and Related Prenatal Care Programs: Interim Report.* Report prepared for the Tennessee Department of Public Health. Arlington, Va.: Wholey Associates, 1981b.

*Joseph S. Wholey is professor of public administration at the University of Southern California and resident at the Washington Public Affairs Center. He was deputy assistant secretary for evaluation in the Department of Health and Human Services from 1978 to 1980 and president of the Evaluation Research Society in 1984.*

*Program theory helps link evaluative information to the creation of important change in social programs.*

# Program Micro- and Macrotheories: A Guide for Social Change

*William R. Shadish, Jr.*

Social program evaluators often claim that the short-term improvement of social programming is one of their primary goals (Cook and Shadish, 1986). The central thesis of this chapter is that any evaluator who endorses such a goal can benefit from program theory. Without program theory, evaluators risk producing information that at best is of unknown relevance to short-term social change and at worst cannot be used for this purpose.

Program theory informs and facilitates social change in two complementary but mutually dependent ways.

1. Program microtheory describes the structural and operational characteristics of what is being evaluated in enough detail to provide information on the general nature of the project or program, its functioning, and (when it is clear that the whole cannot be changed) its changeable component parts.

2. Program macrotheory details the social, psychological, political, organizational, and economic factors that facilitate or constrain change within and outside programs.

Micro- and macrotheories are complementary in that they address orthogonal aspects of program change. Describing the program tells the evaluator

L. Bickman (ed.). *Using Program Theory in Evaluation.*
New Directions for Program Evaluation, no. 33. San Francisco: Jossey-Bass, Spring 1987.

nothing about the likelihood or means of changing the program. But the two kinds of program theory are also mutually dependent in that the worth of each depends on the other. Knowing how to produce change is of less value when one does not also know what the evaluator or the client is trying to change. Hence, both kinds of program theory are essential in evaluation.

Parenthetically, however, although both kinds of theory are important, macrotheory has generally received far less attention from evaluation theorists than has microtheory. For example, Bickman (this volume) notes that all the other chapters in this volume emphasize program microtheory. This leaves macrotheoretical issues about how to produce important social change as the single most important matter that program theory has yet to address in detail.

Of course, evaluators can, and do, quarrel with whether or not the production of short-term social change ought to be a central goal of evaluation (Scriven, 1980). These arguments are credible and reasonable, and will be reviewed later in the chapter. But credible and reasonable arguments can be made on both sides of the issue. For example, since some of the funding for program evaluations depends on the expectation that evaluative information will be useful for such tasks as improving programs and ameliorating social problems, evaluators incur a moral and political obligation to consider social change when they accept such funding. Such change is not all that they must consider, of course, because trade-offs exist between achieving social change and other goals of evaluation.

**The Origins of Program Theory in Evaluation Practice**

It is tempting to think that evaluators, anticipating the difficulties of social change, always use program theory in their work. But some students of the history of science argue that the hypothesis that theory comes first and leads to practice has not generally been true. Rather, as DeMey (1982), they argue that action and technology often precede theory development.

> Kuhn . . . illustrates how up to the nineteenth century a pattern of technology *preceding* science has been the rule. Practical inventions were not the product of applied theoretical science. They resulted from alert handy men who hit upon new combinations of actions and procedures to yield effects that already had some value or that turned out to be valuable. Afterwards, scientists, partly intrigued by some of these results, developed conceptual systems to account for such effects [p. 237].

Program evaluation seems typical of this assertion. It is characterized by an enormous amount of prior application by practical "handymen" aimed at causing program and policy change. Elsewhere, program evaluation has been called "the worldly science" (Cook and Shadish, 1986), in part because its intellectual tasks depend on the challenges provided by a recalcitrant world. In this light, the effort to incorporate program theory into evaluation primarily occurred after rather than before our initial efforts to bring about social change through evaluation over the last twenty years.

Supporting this argument, most of the early work in evaluation (Campbell, 1969; Cronbach, 1963; Scriven, 1967) did not systematically address program theory in the sense described above. In this early work the implicit assumption that social programming could be improved or changed easily was not called into question until the early 1970s, when the results of early evaluations apparently failed to produce program or policy improvement (Weiss, 1973b; Wholey and others, 1970). Then, theorists began to study program theory to help understand and remedy these early failures. Sometimes this study borrowed from literature in a related discipline such as political economy (Lindblom and Cohen, 1979) or implementation theory (Pressman and Wildavsky, 1984). But for the most part, program theory consisted of hunches and intuitions built on common sense and on accumulated professional wisdom and experience about the nature of social programs and how they change.

The study of program theory took two somewhat different directions—what I've referred to as program microtheory and program macrotheory. Both trends remain relatively distinct in evaluation today, an unfortunate occurrence given their mutual dependency. Program microtheories were pursued by theorists such as Wholey, who emphasized the need to construct a model of the program being evaluated in order to know which of its parts were changeable (Horst, Nay, Scanlon, and Wholey, 1974). Theorists who recommend the merits of program microtheory (Chen and Rossi, 1981, 1983; Cronbach, 1982; Stake, 1978; Wholey, 1979) also tend to recommend evaluative practices such as extensive measurement of program implementation, thick description through case studies, and interviews with, or surveys of, program stakeholders.

Program macrotheory, however, is concerned with factors that affect change generally both within and outside programs. Among the earliest evaluators to address this type of program theory was Weiss (1973a, 1973b), who explored the political constraints on program change. Weiss concluded that social systems were remarkably resistent to important social change and that evaluators would for the most part have to be content with conservative, short-term change. This literature was more directly a reaction to difficulties with earlier approaches to evaluation, especially Campbell's (1971) "experimenting society." Such criticisms pointed out that the identification of good solutions to problems was insufficient to ensure that those solutions would be feasible for implementation in society (Shaver and Staines, 1971). Similarly, the ongoing disagreement between

Scriven (1967, 1974, 1980) and Cronbach (1963, 1982) over what relative emphasis to place on summative and formative evaluation, respectively, can be viewed partly as a disagreement about program macrotheory. Scriven argues that summative evaluations help us to know which social interventions should be replaced because they are not valuable, and Cronbach argues that some interventions cannot be replaced because of political reasons, so improving these interventions is the only option.

In the 1980s both types of program theory have become a central part of many prominent approaches to evaluation (Chen and Rossi, 1981, 1983; Cook, Leviton, and Shadish, 1985; Cronbach and others, 1980; Wholey, 1979, 1983). The lessons to be gleaned from this accumulated wisdom are worth reviewing briefly, first, because such a review will provide an overview of the current status of program macrotheory in evaluation and second, because such a review will highlight the central contention in this chapter, namely, that the difficulties of producing important social change warrant more concerted and detailed attention from evaluators.

### Difficulties of Social Change: Program Macrotheory over the Past Twenty Years

Evaluation began during the 1960s, a time when optimism that social problems could be radically ameliorated by social programming was high. Evaluators shared this optimism, assuming that social theory could indicate clear causes of problems as well as powerful solutions, that policymakers would quickly adopt such solutions, and that these solutions would then be implemented by service providers with a resultant significant reduction in problems. But the lessons of the last twenty years make these assumptions questionable. Few theorists are now hopeful that radical amelioration of social problems occurs quickly, easily, or widely. In fact, just the opposite is true: Theorists are most impressed with the conservative nature of social programming and with the difficulties of producing anything but the most incremental changes. Examples of this conservatism include Rossi's (1985) claims that social programs have no effect, Stake and Trumbull's (1982) opinion that local change is mostly incremental, Cronbach and others' (1980) advocacy of marginal changes in programs, Campbell's (1975) dismay about trapped administrators who must maintain program budgets whether or not programs work, Weiss's (1973b) questions about whether basic social research might produce better problem amelioration than evaluation of social programs, Wholey's (1983) comments that dissatisfaction with the performance of government programs abounds, and Scriven's (1967, 1981) concern that stakeholders' anxiety prevents them acting on the results of summative evaluations. From this general agreement on the difficulty of social change follow a host of lessons on why change is so difficult.

*Evaluation Is Dependent on Other Steps in the Social Problem-Solving Process.* Many early evaluation theorists assumed that the major task in social problem solving was simply to identify effective solutions to problems (Campbell, 1969, 1971; Scriven, 1967; Suchman, 1967). Quickly, however, recognition grew that evaluation was dependent on other steps in a problem-solving process that ideally would require that (1) important problems are clearly defined, (2) a wide array of potential solutions is generated, (3) a representative array of these potential solutions are then implemented, (4) these solutions are eventually evaluated, (5) knowledge of the successful solutions is widely disseminated, and (6) powerful stakeholders will use that knowledge in making decisions. Unfortunately, the real world of social programming is not this rational. Problems are ill defined, and stakeholders disagree about the priority each deserves (Bryk, 1983), program objectives are usually vague or contradictory (Wholey, 1983), the change attempts actually implemented on a wide scale are marginal (Shadish, 1984), program structures involve long chains of communication that hinder the accurate dissemination of information among program and project staff (McLaughlin, 1985), and sources of authority for local decision making are typically diffuse and do not just originate as directives from a program central office (Weiss, 1978). Such realities make problematic each step in the formal problem solving process. Technically superior evaluations are ultimately of no more worth than the worst conceived or implemented step in the process.

*Multiple Program Stakeholders Thwart Significant Change.* Another feature of social programs that contributes to minimizing important change is that many different stakeholder groups (Congress, managers, providers, clients) have an interest in most programs. Such stakeholders are politically active, want to see problems formulated in particular ways, and desire particular solutions to those formulations. A proposal must be approved by a majority of these stakeholders to be passed. As a result of these stakeholder interactions, the goals of the program and the proposed means for reaching those goals eventually tend to be conservatively defined in a manner that minimally changes the existing distribution of resources.

Consequently, most programs must have vague goals to accommodate the often conflicting agendas of each group. Hence a concerted attack on a single, clearly defined goal is less likely to give every group its share than is a diffusion of resources. Similarly, proposed solutions must be consistent with majority beliefs about desirable kinds of interventions. But that majority has been socialized to believe in a limited kind of political and economic ideology and social organization (Lindblom, 1977) and is unlikely to approve a program that departs more than marginally from those beliefs. Because ideology and social organization are part of the cause of the problem, working within them is unlikely to produce important changes (Shadish, 1984).

*Social Programs as Heterogeneous Structures.* Another relevant feature of programs that makes it difficult to achieve change is that programs are structurally heterogeneous in implementation across the nation's administrative structure (Lindblom, 1977). Programs are just administrative umbrellas for distributing and regulating funds; they consist of locally implemented projects, where service delivery takes place (Cook, Leviton, and Shadish, 1985). These projects differ widely in character from each other even within the same program, since they are implemented under a national tradition of local control, since service providers often have a tradition of discretion in the services they implement, and since local needs and demands change over place and time. Projects, therefore, consist of an array of different service and administrative elements and are internally heterogeneous as well. Owing to this heterogeneity, services mandated at the program level may or may not be delivered at the local level, and their implementation is at any rate a function of a complex chain of events that cannot be easily controlled by anyone. Planned change is difficult at best under these circumstances.

*Programs as Relatively Permanent Fixtures.* Partly as a result of this better understanding of the structure of social programs, most theorists believe that large social programs (as separate from projects or elements) tend to be relatively permanent fixtures in the policy arena, that such programs certainly do not terminate or begin as a direct result of program evaluation, and that the opportunities for changing programs in the short term tend to occur almost entirely at program margins such as project and element turnover and changing marginal priorities of budget distributions (Kaufman, 1976). As a result, it is more fruitful to attempt to change elements and, occasionally, projects than to try to affect program existence. Hence, even Campbell (1983) recants his former position (Campbell, 1969, 1971) that program funding ought to depend on effective performance as determined by evaluation.

*A Central Paradox in Program Theory.* One of the paradoxes of evaluation is that programs reach more people than do projects, promise larger effects than do individual elements, but are so politically entrenched that they cannot be easily modified by evaluation results. Projects turn over more frequently than programs; by influencing the number and mix of projects in a program, one can influence the program itself. But project turnover is presumably a slow process that can only within limits be speeded up. Elements have potentially the most leverage, since their natural turnover rate is probably the fastest, subject to the provision that they can be added to the repertoires of those who deliver or manage services without much disruption of routine. However, most elements that meet these specifications will usually result in little change in the lives of individual clients. There is a mismatch here between (1) the ability to introduce new practices (lowest with programs and highest with elements),

(2) the number of people who receive new or improved services (lowest with individual projects and highest with programs), and (3) the degree of anticipated influence on individual lives (lowest with individual elements and highest with the combinations of elements usually delivered in programs and projects). Partly owing to this paradox, many differences of opinion arise among evaluation theorists about how evaluation should contribute to social change.

### Prioritizing Incremental Program Improvement

Partly as a result of these lessons, some theorists now argue that special advantages for producing short-term change accrue to social scientists who tie their work to the changes that already take place in society. This generally implies changing elements, or occasionally changing projects, but not changing programs. For example, Lindblom and Cohen (1979) argue that social scientists have no special authority to impose changes on society and so are dependent on naturally occurring changes. Hence, they tell social scientists to study the everyday social interactions of people as they routinely solve their own problems and then to tie change efforts to those existing interactions. Following this rationale, Weiss (1972) advises evaluators first to find out how policy is made and then to tailor evaluations to improving that policymaking process. Wholey (1983) and Stake (1980) tie their work most directly to this kind of incremental change, but Cronbach and others (1980), Weiss (1972), and Berk and Rossi (1976) also prescribe some evaluative activities from this incrementalist mode. *Program improvement* is the term applied to this kind of work.

The resulting changes are more frequent and feasible than are efforts to change programs themselves. This situation is partly due to the fact that program turnover is rarer than project or element turnover, but it is also because efforts to work within the status quo are more likely to gain the support of the majority of stakeholders who helped initially develop the program. Evaluators are more likely to receive financial and moral support from powerful program stakeholders if they try to improve program performance rather than if they attack the fundamental assumptions of the program and call for its replacement. Since evaluators are primarily professionals who depend on stakeholder support for their livelihood, improvement of program performance must be a central focus if the profession is to remain viable (Shadish, 1986).

### Evaluation and Short-Term Change

Partly because of these very strengths, program improvement is more conservative and incremental than some evaluators would like it to be. For example, although recognizing that studying such incremental change is probably more likely to affect practice in the short term, Campbell (1971) still focuses attention on demonstrations of the effectiveness of novel interventions that differ from existing policies and programs in important ways. He reasons that because society does not generally generate novel options due to its conservative nature, it is in the generation and evaluation of such options that the evaluator can be of most service (Campbell, 1977).

Similarly, Scriven (1980) believes that real improvement results from adopting solutions that meet important social needs. Both authors would presumably favor a single rare but novel change that accomplished this end rather than many incremental changes that are so similar to past interventions that little real change occurs. Although Campbell (1983) is especially sensitive to the fact that program turnover is less likely than project or element turnover, both authors would agree on a focus on program change and an emphasis on identifying solutions to social problems no matter what level of the program was studied.

Perhaps more important, both Campbell and Scriven might question the fundamental assumption in this chapter that buttresses the presumed need for program theory, namely, that evaluators should prioritize producing social change. To these authors, evaluation should aim not so much at producing social change as at informing society whether the interventions are effective or good. This means that short-term change is of secondary importance compared to the critical examination of program effectiveness and value. If the program is fundamentally flawed, program improvement is at best a purposeless exercise and at worst a self-serving political and economic strategy that becomes seriously compromised when it joins forces with the very social institutions it is supposed to evaluate. Someone must have the courage to say that the program has no merit!

Lest we dismiss such a position as naive ivory-tower rhetoric, it is worth noting similar pleas from an experienced civil servant who is quite sensitive to political and economic realities. In a plenary address to the 1985 annual meeting of the Evaluation Research Society/Evaluation Network, Canadian Comptroller General Michael Rayner praised evaluators for their many contributions to program improvement but also admonished them for not making hard judgments about which programs worked and which did not (Rayner, 1986). In another plenary address the following day, Scriven reminded his audience that one of the most politically effective evaluations of this decade, by Charles Murray (1984), was essentially a summative evaluation aimed not at improving existing social welfare programs but at rendering the judgment that the social welfare policies of the last thirty years did not work (Scriven, 1986). Both Rayner and Scriven make the point that evaluation must be able to make value judgments that are not contingent on short-term use. In the headlong rush to produce usable evaluative information, evaluation must be careful not to throw out the baby (social criticism) with the bathwater (the difficulties encountered in producing short-term uses when doing social criticism).

The critical question is how to find a realistic role for the type of evaluation advocated by Campbell and Scriven. Undoubtedly, some evaluators are in better positions than others to make hard-hitting social criticism. Evaluators who work directly for the program being evaluated or who have a contract from the organization are pressured to avoid trenchant questions (Cook and Shadish, 1982; Flaherty and Windle, 1981; Kennedy, 1983; Peck and Rubin, 1983). For most practicing evaluators, the choice of work within the status quo may not only be what clients want but may also be the only feasible option given the politics and economics of evaluation practice (Shadish, 1986).

These circumstances make it easier to understand Scriven's (1976) point that the evaluator has independent financial and organizational status from the program being evaluated. This desire reflects Scriven's underlying wish that the evaluator, as a social critic, be free from practical constraints. But unlike program improvement, there are few willing to foot the bill for social criticism. For the present such critical evaluation will remain the province of two separate groups. The first group is academic evaluators, who are less likely to be pressured to produce results of short-term usefulness or to be organizationally subservient to the entity being evaluated. The second group consists of evaluators in organizations such as the U.S. General Accounting Office (GAO), which has a political mandate to criticize social programs and policies. Although Congress may constrain such organizations as GAO somewhat more than academic evaluators, this disadvantage may be offset by the fact that GAO usually has more resources and political clout in conducting and implementing evaluations.

Both of these groups therefore play complementary roles in social criticism and can plausibly do so more than can most agency evaluators and contract research firms. The more difficult question is whether or not it is either possible or desirable for such agency evaluators to engage in even more social criticism. Evaluators in more constrained positions would be unlikely to succeed in unilaterally changing current practice by being more critical. They do not have the authority for such criticism, and their attempts would probably be opposed by those who do have authority. Since it is likely that there will always be some evaluators willing to perform in a conventional manner, it would be economically foolhardy to take such a critical stance (Shadish, 1986).

If there is to be change, it might come from two somewhat unlooked-for directions. The first source of change could come from compelling demonstrations by evaluators of the immediate usefulness of evaluations that focus more on the summative than the formative. Such studies as Murray's (1984) critique of the welfare state should be examined in order to understand why it is apparently successful in contributing to current efforts to dismantle much of social programming. Is it successful because it questions fundamental assumptions, calls for sweeping changes, is data based, accidentally coincides with a sympathetic administration, or all these? A second course would be to examine the role that could be played by summative evaluations that do not call for such fundamental and sweeping changes (Cook, 1984). An example might be the apparent usefulness and popularity in policy circles of metaanalyses that examine, for instance, which psychotherapies work (Smith, Glass, and Miller, 1980).

The second source for change lies in the political and economic environment of the programs themselves. Massive federal budget cuts, such as those proposed under the Gramm-Rudman-Hollings amendment, might force federal policymakers to make hard choices about which programs are to be cut and by how much. Summative evaluation will never determine such changes entirely, but it can serve as an important source of input that would be more valued in such a fiscal environment—particularly if evaluators can anticipate which programs are likely candidates and prepare timely summative evaluations of them prior to the decision (Shadish, 1984). But even in this scenario, it is unlikely that evaluators who work for the organization being evaluated will produce accurate summative evaluations. It is more likely that they will be under considerable pressure to show that their program is the one that should be retained.

In summary, theorists such as Scriven (1980, 1986) argue reasonably that evaluation should tell society which of its programs are good. This point is well taken; undoubtedly some evaluators have unwittingly sacrificed the social significance of their work to the shibboleth of short-term use (Cook and Shadish, 1982). These evaluators must find ways to bring value back into evaluation. But Scriven (and Campbell) must bring program theory back into their versions of evaluation, at least where they want evaluators to contribute to short-term change. Two conclusions seem warranted: First, evaluators must stop writing as if all program evaluators should take either one or the other stance. In a profession as large and as diverse as evaluation, it is appropriate that tasks and goals be diverse and reflect both the logic of the field and the constraints and opportunities within which different evaluators work. Second, evaluators must continue to find new ways to ameliorate the trade-off between achieving short-term social change and providing fundamental social criticism of social interventions. In this task lies the most important challenges to program theory. Although it is unlikely that there are ways to resolve the dilemma completely, the gap might nonetheless be closed somewhat; any practical help in resolving this problem is a step in the right direction, such as the following example illustrates.

### An Example of Important Short-Term Changes
### that Were Widely Implemented

For both political and economic reasons, most evaluators will probably choose to work within the assumptions and dictates of current programs and policies (Shadish, 1986). Short-term incremental changes will be the primary goal of such evaluators. Most often this will involve a focus on program and project elements; given the rapidity of their naturally occurring turnover, these elements offer the most frequently occurring opportunities for incremental change. But since replacing such elements is most likely to lead to changes that are small and incremental rather than novel and important, theorists must identify attributes of those interventions that are most likely to make them both feasible and important in producing significant change. One way to do this is to study past policy innovations with various combinations of these attributes.

In a recent article that begins to illustrate this kind of analysis, I contrasted the relative fates of Fairweather's (1980) Lodge Society with the nursing home industry as care sites for the chronically mentally ill (Shadish, 1984). Evaluations of the lodge were summative, explicitly modelled after Campbell's experimenting society, and showed that the lodge solved most of the problems that led to deinstitutionalization. But the lodge plan is not widely implemented. In contrast, nursing homes are widely implemented but do not solve most of the problems that led to deinstitutionalization. This observation, moreover, is not specific to the lodge and the nursing home industry but extends to other innovative care programs (Kiesler, 1982; Stein and Test, 1978) and to other industries that resemble nursing homes, such as the board-and-care home industry (Segal and Aviram, 1978). The conclusion in the Shadish (1984) article was that any proposed policy innovation must be consistent with the ideologies and social structures of the social system that must implement it. Since the lodge plan does not have this consistency but the nursing home industry does, only the latter was widely implemented. Policy, it seems, is more responsive to structural and ideological consistency than to success at solving social problems.

But for present purposes, the Shadish analysis is incomplete—it did not examine innovations that solved the problems that led to deinstitutionalization and were widely implemented or that neither solved the problems nor were implemented. A next step might be a series of exploratory case studies that examine the properties of multiple innovations as shown in Figure 1. The figure has four cells that result from the conjunction of two factors—whether or not an innovation solved the problems at issue and whether or not it was widely implemented. Examination of the characteristics of examples from each cell would presumably help identify characteristics of each kind of success and failure. Fairweather's Lodge is illustrated in the lower-left corner cell of Figure 1 and the nursing home industry illustrated the upper-right corner cell. The Fairweather case study helped to highlight the critical importance of an implementability factor in program evaluations—successful policy innovations must not only improve problem amelioration but must also be implementable.

But presumably it is the upper-left corner cell that is the ideal goal of evaluation—to aid in identifying implementable solutions. Two examples that might fall into that cell are the use of phenothiazine medications for treating psychotic disorders and the use of systematic desensitization for treating phobias. What characteristics of these innovations allowed them to be both implementable and successful? Regarding their implementability, for example, each is a manipulable practice (Campbell, 1969), difficult to implement incorrectly (Sechrest and others, 1979), consonant with the values and practices of the professionals who use it (Fullan, 1982), keyed to an easily identified problem (Williams, 1980), reasonably inexpensive (Cook, 1982), and somewhat robust in effects across different types of clients and service providers (Cook and others, 1985). Regarding their success as solutions to problems, each can be used to influence many lives, will significantly ameliorate patient needs, and will demonstrably lead to enhanced functioning by reasonable criteria (Cook, 1982). With an expanded and cross-validated list of such characteristics, evaluators could begin to anticipate which innovations are worth studying because they fit the profile of interventions that might be both successful and implementable.

These comments illustrate the kind of discovery-oriented case studies suggested by Figure 1. The importance of such studies lies in their potential contribution to resolving the apparent paradox noted several times now in this chapter, namely, that innovations are more implementable to the extent that they preserve the status quo but thus also tend to contribute minimally to the solution of problems that are themselves a product of that status quo (Shadish, 1984). Resolving this paradox may be the central challenge to program theory that emerges from the last twenty years of evaluation practice.

## Conclusion

Many evaluators are only haphazardly aware of existing literature relevant to program theory. For example, Pressman and Wildavsky's (1984) study of the implementation of a project in Oakland has become a minor classic in our field. A great deal more can be learned by seeking out literature on social change. Even a cursory examination reveals plausibly relevant work in such areas as large-scale social change (Chirot, 1977; Fals Borda, 1985), social action (Adler, 1981), social movements (Jenckins, 1983), political economy (Lindblom, 1977), political innovation (Polsby, 1984), organizational development and change (Huse, 1975), organizational performance (Kanter and Brinkerhoff, 1981), policy formulation and imple-

**Figure 1. A Framework for Case Studies of Important Social Changes**

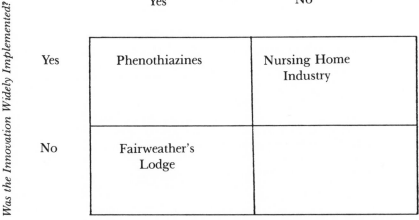

mentation (Brigham and Brown, 1980; May and Wildavsky, 1978), public interest law (Weisbrod, Handler, and Komesar, 1978), and public administration (Gould, 1979). Further, to the extent that evaluation training programs have required evaluation courses, such literature ought to be required reading in a course on program theory.

Earlier in this chapter, we quoted DeMey's (1982) remark to the effect that theory development follows practice. If so, then we now have twenty years of evaluation practice on which to reflect as we build program theory. Given the breadth of disciplines contributing to the literature, program theorists would be well advised to take a multidisciplinary perspective. Many obstacles might impede evaluators who wish to take up this gauntlet. These include, for example, pressures to conform to disciplinary dogma and difficulties locating and mastering literatures written from diverse paradigms of theory and method. But these impediments notwithstanding, if evaluation is to advance intellectually as a discipline, this is one of the central challenges it must address (Cook and Shadish, 1986). Few other disciplines face this important challenge; of those that do, fewer still have both the interdisciplinary resources and the practical experience of social change that evaluation possesses. Opportunity knocks at our door. Will we answer?

**References**

Adler, P. *Momentum: A Theory of Social Action.* Beverly Hills, Calif.: Sage, 1981.

Berk, R. A., and Rossi, P. H. "Doing Good or Worse: Evaluation Research Politically Reexamined." *Social Problems,* 1976, *23,* 337–349.

Brigham, J., and Brown, D. W. (eds.). *Policy Implementation: Penalties or Incentives.* Beverly Hills, Calif.: Sage, 1980.

Bryk, A. S. (ed.). *Stakeholder-Based Evaluation.* New Directions for Program Evaluation, no. 17. San Francisco: Jossey-Bass, 1983.

Campbell, D. T. "Reforms as Experiments." *American Psychologist,* 1969, *24,* 409-429.

Campbell, D. T. *Methods for the Experimenting Society.* Paper presented to the Eastern Psychological Association, New York City, and to the American Psychological Association, Washington, D.C., 1971.

Campbell, D. T. "Assessing the Impact of Planned Social Change." In G. M. Lyons (ed.), *Social Research and Public Policies.* Hanover, N.H.: Public Affairs Center, Dartmouth College, 1975.

Campbell, D. T. *Descriptive Epistemology: Psychological, Sociological, and Evolutionary.* William James Lectures. Cambridge, Mass.: Harvard University, 1977.

Campbell, D. T. *The Problem of Being Scientific in Program Evaluation, Considered in the Light of an Epistemological Sociology of Science.* Paper presented at the Evaluation Research Society, Chicago, Illinois, 1983.

Chen, H.-T., and Rossi, P. H. "The Multi-Goal, Theory-Driven Approach to Evaluation: A Model Linking Basic and Applied Social Science." In H. E. Freeman and M. A. Solomon (eds.), *Evaluation Studies Review Annual.* Vol. 6. Beverly Hills, Calif.: Sage, 1981.

Chen, H.-T., and Rossi, P. H. "Evaluating with Sense: The Theory-Driven Approach." *Evaluation Review,* 1983, *7,* 283-302.

Chirot, D. *Social Change in the Twentieth Century.* San Diego, Calif.: Harcourt Brace Jovanovich, 1977.

Cook, F. L. "Assessing Age as an Eligibility Criterion." In B. L. Neugarten (ed.), *Age or Need? Public Policies for Older People.* Beverly Hills, Calif.: Sage, 1982.

Cook, T. D. "Opportunities for Evaluation in the Next Few Years." *Evaluation News,* 1984, *5,* 20-46.

Cook, T. D., Leviton, L. C., and Shadish, W. R., Jr. "Program Evaluation." In G. Lindzey and E. Aronson (eds.), *Handbook of Social Psychology.* (3rd ed.) New York: Random House, 1985.

Cook, T. D., and Shadish, W. R., Jr. "Metaevaluation: An Evaluation of the Congressionally Mandated Evaluation System for Community Mental Health Centers." In G. Stahler and W. R. Tash (eds.), *Innovative Approaches to Mental Health Evaluation.* Orlando, Fla.: Academic Press, 1982.

Cook, T. D., and Shadish, W. R., Jr. "Program Evaluation: The Worldly Science." *Annual Review of Psychology,* 1986, *37,* 193-232.

Cronbach, L. J. "Course Improvement Through Evaluation." *Teachers College Record,* 1963, *64,* 672-683.

Cronbach, L. J. *Designing Evaluations of Educational and Social Programs.* San Francisco: Jossey-Bass, 1982.

Cronbach, L. J., Ambron, S. R., Dornbusch, S. M., Hess, R. D., Hornik, R. C., Phillips, D. C., Walker, D. F., and Weiner, S. S. *Toward Reform of Program Evaluation.* San Francisco: Jossey-Bass, 1980.

DeMey, M. *The Cognitive Paradigm.* Dordrecht, Holland: D. Reidel, 1982.

Fairweather, G. W. *The Fairweather Lodge: A Twenty-Five Year Retrospective.* New Directions for Mental Health Services, no. 7. San Francisco: Jossey-Bass, 1980.

Fals Borda, O. (ed.). *The Challenge of Social Change.* Beverly Hills, Calif.: Sage, 1985.

Flaherty, E. W., and Windle, C. "Mandated Evaluation in Community Mental

Health Centers: Framework for a New Policy." *Evaluation Review,* 1981, *5,* 620–638.

Fullan, M. *The Meaning of Educational Change.* New York: Teachers College Press, 1982.

Gould, D. J. *Law and the Administrative Process: Analytic Frameworks for Understanding Public Policymaking.* Washington, D.C.: University Press of America, 1979.

Horst, P., Nay, J. N., Scanlon, J. W., and Wholey, J. S. "Program Management and the Federal Evaluator." *Public Administration Review,* 1974, *34,* 300–308.

Huse, E. F. *Organizational Development and Change.* St. Paul, Minn.: West, 1975.

Jenckins, J. C. "Resource Mobilization Theory and the Study of Social Movement." *Annual Review of Sociology,* 1983, *9,* 527–533.

Kanter, R. M., and Brinkerhoff, D. "Organizational Performance: Recent Developments in Measurement." *Annual Review of Sociology,* 1981, *7,* 321–349.

Kaufman, H. *Are Government Organizations Immortal?* Washington, D.C.: Brookings Institution, 1976.

Kennedy, M. M. "The Role of the In-House Evaluator." *Evaluation Review,* 1983, *7,* 519–542.

Kiesler, C. A. "Mental Hospitals and Alternative Care: Noninstitutionalization as a Potential Public Policy for Mental Patients." *American Psychologist,* 1982, *37,* 349–360.

Lindblom, C. E. *Politics and Markets: The World's Political Economic Systems.* New York: Basic Books, 1977.

Lindblom, C. E., and Cohen, D. K. *Usable Knowledge: Social Science and Social Problem Solving.* New Haven, Conn.: Yale University Press, 1979.

McLaughlin, M. W. "Implementation Realities and Evaluation Design." In R. L. Shotland and M. M. Mark (eds.), *Social Science and Social Policy.* Beverly Hills, Calif.: Sage, 1985.

May, J. V., and Wildavsky, A. B. (eds.). *The Policy Cycle.* Beverly Hills, Calif.: Sage, 1978.

Murray, C. *Losing Ground: American Social Policy, 1950–1980.* New York: Basic Books, 1984.

Peck, D. L., and Rubin, H. J. "Bureaucratic Needs and Evaluation Research: A Case Study of the Department of Housing and Urban Development." *Evaluation Review,* 1983, *7,* 685–703.

Polsby, N. W. *Political Innovation in America: The Politics of Policy Initiation.* New Haven, Conn.: Yale University Press, 1984.

Pressman, J. L., and Wildavsky, A. *Implementation.* (3rd ed.) Berkeley: University of California Press, 1984.

Rayner, M. "Evaluation in Canada." *Evaluation Practice,* 1986, *7,* 45–56.

Rossi, P. H. *The Iron Law of Evaluation and Other Metallic Rules.* Paper presented at Rockefeller College, SUNY-Albany, Albany, New York, April 17, 1985.

Scriven, M. "The Methodology of Evaluation." In R. E. Stake and others (eds.), *Perspectives on Curriculum Evaluation.* AERA Monograph Series on Curriculum Evaluation, no. 1. Skokie, Ill.: Rand McNally, 1967.

Scriven, M. "Evaluation Perspectives and Procedures." In J. W. Popham (ed.), *Evaluation in Education: Current Application.* Berkeley, Calif.: McCutchan, 1974.

Scriven, M. "Evaluation Bias and Its Control." In G. V. Glass (ed.), *Evaluation Studies Review Annual.* Vol. 1. Beverly Hills, Calif.: Sage, 1976.

Scriven, M. *The Logic of Evaluation.* Inverness, Calif.: Edgepress, 1980.

Scriven, M. "Product Evaluation." In N. L. Smith (ed.), *New Techniques for Evaluation.* Beverly Hills, Calif.: Sage, 1981.

Scriven, M. "New Frontiers in Evaluation." *Evaluation Practice*, 1986, 7, 7–44.

Sechrest, L., West, S. G., Phillips, M. A., Redner, R., and Yeaton, W. (eds.). *Evaluation Studies Review Annual*. Vol. 4. Beverly Hills, Calif.: Sage, 1979.

Segal, S. P., and Aviram, U. *The Mentally Ill in Community-Based Sheltered Care*. New York: Wiley, 1978.

Shadish, W. R., Jr. "Policy Research: Lessons from the Implementation of Deinstitutionalization." *American Psychologist*, 1984, *39*, 725–738.

Shadish, W. R., Jr. "Sources of Evaluation Practice: Needs, Purposes, Questions, and Technology." In L. Bickman and D. L. Weatherford (eds.), *Evaluating Early Interventions Programs for Severely Handicapped Children and Their Families*. Austin, Tex.: Pro-Ed, 1986.

Shaver, P., and Staines, G. "Problems Facing Campbell's 'Experimenting Society.' " *Urban Affairs Quarterly*, 1971, 7, 173–186.

Smith, M. L., Glass, G. V., and Miller, T. I. *The Benefits of Psychotherapy*. Baltimore: Johns Hopkins University Press, 1980.

Stake, R. E. "The Case Study Method in Social Inquiry." *Educational Research*, 1978, 7, 5–8.

Stake, R. E. "Quality of Education and the Dimunition of Local Control in Schools in the United States." In *Needs of Elementary and Secondary Education in the 1980s*. Committee on Education and Labor, U.S. House of Representatives. Washington, D.C.: U.S. Government Printing Office, 1980.

Stake, R. E., and Trumbull, D. J. "Naturalistic Generalizations." *Review Journal of Philosophy and Social Science*, 1982, 7, 1–12.

Stein, L. I., and Test, M. A. *Alternatives to Mental Hospital Treatment*. New York: Plenum, 1978.

Suchman, E. A. *Evaluative Research: Principles and Practice in Public Service and Social Action Programs*. New York: Russell Sage, 1967.

Weisbrod, B. A., Handler, J. F., and Komesar, N. K. *Public Interest Law: An Economic and Institutional Analysis*. Berkeley: University of California Press, 1978.

Weiss, C. H. *Evaluation Research: Methods for Assessing Program Effectiveness*. Englewood Cliffs, N.J.: Prentice-Hall, 1972.

Weiss, C. H. "The Politics of Impact Measurement." *Policy Studies Journal*, 1973a, *1*, 179–183.

Weiss, C. H. "Where Politics and Evaluation Research Meet." *Evaluation*, 1973b, *1*, 37–45.

Weiss, C. H. "Improving the Linkage Between Social Research and Public Policy." In L. E. Lynn (ed.), *Knowledge and Policy: The Uncertain Connection*. Washington, D.C.: National Academy of Sciences, 1978.

Wholey, J. S. *Evaluation: Promise and Performance*. Washington, D.C.: Urban Institute, 1979.

Wholey, J. S. *Evaluation and Effective Public Management*. Boston: Little, Brown, 1983.

Wholey, J. S., Scanlon, J. W., Duffy, H. G., Fukumoto, J. S., and Vogt, L. M. *Federal Evaluation Policy: Analyzing the Effects of Public Programs*. Washington, D.C.: Urban Institute, 1970.

Williams, W. *The Implementation Perspective*. Berkeley: University of California Press, 1980.

*William R. Shadish, Jr., is associate professor, Center for Applied Psychological Research in the psychology department, Memphis State University. His current interests include social change, where he has focused primarily on the intractable problems posed by the chronically mentally ill, and metascience, particularly in the context of his interest in evaluation theory. His work on these topics has appeared in the* Annual Review of Psychology, *the* Handbook of Social Psychology, *the* Evaluation Studies Review Annual, *and the* American Psychologist.

# Index

## A

Acker, N., 32, 41
Adler, P., 104, 105
Adolescents: with behavioral disorders, 30–36; prenatal program for, 81–85
Adult Day Care Assessment Procedure (ADCAP), 37–39
Adult Day Health Care (ADHC), and program philosophy, 36–39
Aid Association for Lutherans (AAL): Co-op Benevolence Program of, 87; evaluability assessment of fraternal benefit program for, 86–90, 91; Fraternal and Benevolence Committee of, 86, 87, 89
Alexander, E. R., 43, 56
Ambron, S. R., 106
American Association of Retired Persons, 39
Anderson, C. A., 14, 16
Andrus Foundation, 39
Apter, S. J., 32, 33n, 40
Assessment. *See* Evaluability assessment
Avellar, J. W., 76
Aviram, U., 103, 108
Axelrod, R., 51, 56

## B

Bandura, A., 7, 17
Bardach, E., 73, 75
Bateman, P. M., 64, 76
Bell, J. B., 78, 92
Bellavita, C., 77n
Berk, R. A., 99, 105
Berman, P., 61, 70, 75
Beyer, J. M., 68, 75
Bickel, K. L., 86, 88n, 91–92
Bickman, L., 2, 3, 5, 6, 7, 9, 10, 11, 12, 14, 17, 18, 19n, 21, 40, 43n, 45, 50, 56, 59n, 77n, 94
Blakely, C., 65, 70, 75
Boudreau, J. W., 55, 56

Bougon, M. G., 15, 18
Boylan, M. G., 76
Brazil, squatter settlements in, 46
Brenner, M., 15, 17
Brickman, P., 22, 23, 40
Bridging variables, concept of, 12
Brigham, J., 105, 106
Brinkerhoff, D., 104, 107
Brown, D. W., 105, 106
Brown, G., 31, 40
Brown, J., 15, 17
Brunsson, N., 50, 56
Bryk, A. S., 62, 75, 97, 106
Bureau of Educationally Handicapped, 31

## C

California at Los Angeles, University of, Department of Medicine, 37, 42
Cameron, K., 54, 56
Campbell, D. T., 7, 8, 16, 17, 20, 21, 30, 40, 95, 96, 97, 98, 100, 101, 102, 103, 104, 106
Canter, D., 15, 17, 49, 56
Causal modeling, and action heuristics, 51–54
Change. *See* Social change
Chelimsky, E., 64, 75
Chen, H.-T., 6, 7, 14, 17, 20, 21, 22, 40, 95, 96, 106
Chicago Child Parent Center Program, 24
Chirot, D., 104, 106
Clients, and implementation, 70
Coates, D., 40
Cohen, D. K., 95, 99, 107
Cohn, E., 40
Colton, R. M., 61, 75
Community Mental Health Center Program, 24
Component assessment, and action heuristics, 50
Concept clarification, and conceptual heuristics, 47–48
Conceptual maps: and conceptual

Conceptual maps *(continued)*
    heuristics, 49; for program philoso-
    phy, 31–33
Congress, 97
Conrad, K. J., 1, 5, 13, 15, 19, 30, 37,
    39, 40 42, 50
Consensus: and program philosophy,
    31, 37; and program theory, 13
Cook, F. L., 104, 106
Cook, T. D., 7, 8, 16, 17, 21, 23, 24, 40,
    93, 95, 96, 98, 101, 102, 104, 105, 106
Cooley, W. W., 22, 40
Cost-benefit analysis, and action heu-
    ristics, 54
Cronbach, L. J., 6, 8, 17, 95, 96, 99,
    106
Crosse, S., 17, 75
Crovitz, H. F., 48, 56

**D**

Data analysis, for program philoso-
    phy, 32–36
Davidson, W., II, 75
Decision analysis, and action heuris-
    tics, 54–55
Delbec, A. L., 44, 56
DeMey, M., 94, 105, 106
Department of Finance and Adminis-
    tration (Tennessee), 82
Department of Public Health (Tennes-
    see), 81, 82, 84, 85
Dornbusch, S. M., 106
Duffy, H. G., 108
Dunkle, J., 17, 75

**E**

Eash, M., 19*n*, 30, 40
Eden, C., 51, 52, 56
Education for All Handicapped Chil-
    dren Act of 1975 (PL 94-142), 31
Edwards, J., 10, 17
Elements: concept of, 24; in macrothe-
    ory, 98–99; and service goals, 27
Ellickson, P., 68, 75
Elmore, R. F., 63, 75
Emsoff, J., 75
Environment, and implementation,
    73–74
Erlebacher, A., 30, 40
*Estate of Smith* v. *M. Heckler*, 21, 40
Evaluability assessment: and action
heuristics, 50; analysis of, 77–92;
    background on, 77–78; and clarify-
    ing uses of evaluation, 78–81; con-
    cept of, 78; context of, 86; examples
    of, 81–90; involvement in, 79; pro-
    cess and products of, 82–84, 86–88;
    results of, 84–85, 89–90; significance
    of, 90–91
Evaluation: barriers to use of, 77–78,
    90–91; clarifying uses of, 81; depen-
    dency of, 97; formative, 12–13, 43,
    44–46; origins of program theory in,
    94–96; and short-term change,
    99–102; and social change, 93–109;
    stages of, and program philosophy,
    28–30
Evaluators: conceptual and action heu-
    ristics for, 43–57; and implementa-
    tion process theory, 59–76; roles of,
    62–63, 65, 67
Eveland, J. D., 70, 75, 76
Exemplary Projects Program, 65
Ezrahi, Y., 23, 40

**F**

Fairweather, G. W., 76, 103, 104, 105,
    106
Fals Borda, O., 104, 106
Fault trees, and action heuristics, 54
Fergus, E. O., 76
Fischoff, B., 14, 18
Flaherty, E. W., 101, 106–107
Fleischer, M., 76
Follow Through Program, and pro-
    gram philosophy, 20
Formative evaluation: objective of, 43;
    and program theory, 12–13; and
    uncertainty, 44–46
Forrester, J. W., 55, 56
Freeman, H. E., 46, 57
Fukumoto, J. S., 108
Fullan, M., 104, 107

**G**

Gaertner, G. H., 76
General Accounting Office, 64, 101
Generalizability, and policymaking,
    8–9
Glaser, B. G., 90, 92
Glass, G. V., 102, 108

Goals, and program philosophy, 27-28
Gottschalk, R., 755
Gould, D. J., 105, 107
Governor's Task Force on Mental Retardation (Tennessee), 85
Gowin, D. B., 49, 56
Gramm-Rudman-Hollings amendment, 102
Greene, J., 43$n$
Greer, A. L., 72, 75
Groat, L., 15, 17
Gurel, L., 22, 41

**H**

Hackman, J. R., 25, 40-41
Haertel, G., 19$n$
Hall, R. I., 51, 57
Handler, J. F., 105, 108
Haney, W., 20, 41
Hansberry Child Parent Center, 24
Hare, A. P., 22, 23, 24, 25, 41
Head Start Program: and measurement issues, 13; and program philosophy, 20, 24, 30
Hedrick, S. C., 41
Hess, R. D., 106
Hetzner, W. A., 76
Heuristics: action, 45, 50-55; analysis of, 43-57; applications of, 45; background on, 43-44; conceptual, 45, 46-49; conclusion on, 55; and formative evaluation, 44-46
Hornik, R. C., 106
Horst, P., 77, 92, 95, 107
Hotch, D., 10, 17
House, E. R., 46, 47, 56
Hughes, S. L., 39, 40
Huse, E. F., 104, 107

**I**

Illinois, survey of programs in, 32
Implementation: and action heuristics, 50; concept of, 61; and program theory, 11-12; of social change, 103-105; testing, 28, 29, 36-39
Implementation process theory: analysis of, 59-76; and assessing extent of implementation, 61-66; background on, 59-61; and clients, 70; concept of, 60; conclusions on, 74-75; and environment, 73-74; issues in, 66-74; methodology for, 68; and organizational structures, 72-73; and program, 70; and program deliverers, 70-72; and social system perspective and components, 69-74; summary on, 66, 67, 74; and work units, 72
Intentions, at program level, 27
Intervening variables, and program theory, 12
Inui, T. S., 41

**J**

Janis, I. L., 14, 17
Jenckins, J. C., 104, 107
Johnson, B. M., 66, 72, 75
Johnson, E. C., 76
Jones, S., 51, 52, 56
Judd, C. M., 29, 41

**K**

Kanter, R. M., 104, 107
Karuza, J., Jr., 40
Kaufman, H., 98, 107
Kay, P., 78, 92
Kennedy, M. M., 101, 107
Kenny, D. A., 29, 41
Kidder, L., 40
Kiesler, C. A., 103, 107
Klepper, C. A., 70, 75
Komesar, N. K., 105, 108
Kravitz, D. A., 22, 41
Kuhn, T., 94

**L**

Leavitt, H. J., 43, 56
Lemke, S., 21, 36, 37, 39, 41
Lepper, M. R., 14, 17
Lerman, P., 46-47, 56
Levin, H. M., 54, 56
Leviton, L. C., 8, 17, 21, 23, 24, 40, 96, 98, 106
Lindblom, C. E., 95, 97, 98, 99, 104, 107
Linn, B. S., 22, 41
Linn, M. W., 22, 41
Lipsey, M. W., 10, 15-16, 17, 66, 75
Lipsky, M. W., 45, 56, 71, 76
Lohnes, P. R., 22, 40

Lord, C. G., 14, 17
Louis, K. S., 68, 72, 76

**M**

McClintock, C., 1, 5, 12, 15, 43, 44, 50, 56, 57, 59n
McDaniels, G. L., 20, 41
McGrath, J. E., 20, 22, 23, 25n, 41
McKinlay, J. B., 72, 76
McLaughlin, M. W., 70, 75, 97, 107
Macroimplementation: measuring, 63-64, 67; perspective of, 61-62, 68
Macrotheory: concept of, 6, 93; and difficulties of social change, 96-99; trends in, 95-96
McSwain, C., 77n
Mann, L., 14, 17
Mapping sentences, and conceptual heuristics, 49
Mark, M. M., 45, 57, 62, 76
Marks, E. L., 64, 76
Marquart, J., 43n
Mauser, A. J., 31, 42
May, J. V., 105, 107
Mayer, J., 75
Maynard-Moddy, S., 44, 56
Mazmanian, D., 63, 76
Means, testing, 28, 29, 36-39
Measurement, issues of, and program theory, 13
Medicaid, 21, 85
Medicare, 21
Medley, D. M., 19, 41
Metaphors, and conceptual heuristics, 46-47
Microimplementation: measuring, 64-66, 67; perspective of, 61-62, 68
Microtheory: concept of, 5-6, 93; and social science knowledge, 8; trends in, 95
Miller, T. I., 102, 108
Miller, T. Q., 1, 15, 19, 37, 40, 42, 50
Mitzel, H. E., 19, 41
Moos, R. H., 21, 22, 36, 37, 39, 41
Morris, G. G., 25, 40-41
Morse, W. C., 32, 41
Murray, C., 100, 102, 107

**N**

Nagel, S. S., 55, 56
National Diffusion Network, 65

National Institute of Dental Research, 59n
National Science Foundation, 68; Innovation Centers Program of, 61-62
Nay, J. N., 77, 78, 92, 95, 107
Newman, P. D., 76
Nieva, V. F., 76
Nixon administration, 30
Nocera, C., 43n
North Memphis Community Mental Health Center, 24
Novak, J. D., 49, 56
Nursing homes, quality of, 22-22, 103-104

**O**

Ohio University, 42
Organizations, and implementation, 72-73

**P**

Packer, M. J., 47, 57
Palmer, D., 31, 40
Parsons, T., 22-23, 41
Peck, D. L., 101, 107
Perlman, J., 46, 57
Petersilia, J., 68, 75
Phillips, D. C., 106
Phillips, M. A., 108
Philosophy. See Program philosophy
Policymaking, and program theory, 8-10
Pollard, J., 17, 75
Polsby, N. W., 104, 107
Pressman, J. L., 28, 41, 45, 57, 63, 68, 76, 95, 104, 107
Problem, and target group, and program theory, 11
Program: concept of, 24, 61, 78; deliverers of, 70-72; development model for, 25-28; failure of, 10-11; as heterogeneous, 98; and implementation, 70; incremental improvement of, 99; and intentions, 27; in macrotheory, 98-99; permanency of, 98
Program philosophy: analysis of, 19-42; concept of, 5; and consensus, 31, 37; data analysis for, 32-36; defi-

nition needed for, 30-36; definitions and assumptions in, 22-24; and evaluation stages, 29-30; examples of, 20, 30-39; history of, 19-22; measuring, 28, 29; need to measure, 24-25; and program development model, 25-28; recent developments in, 20-22; recommendations on, 39; results of defining, 36-39; testing, 28, 29-30; and values, 22-23

Program theory: analysis of, 5-18; for assessing extent of implementation, 61-66; clarifying, 79-80; concepts of, 5-6, 43, 60-61, 78-79; and conceptual and action heuristics, 43-57; and consensus, 13; development of, 13-16, 78-81; and evaluability assessment, 77-92; in evaluation, 94-96; failure of, and program failure, 10-11; and formative evaluation, 12-13; functions of, 6-13; and implementation process theory, 11-12, 59-76; implicit to explicit, 14-15; and intervening variables, 12; and measurement issues, 13; micro- and macro-, 93-109; paradox in, 98-99; and philosophy, 19-42; and policymaking, 8-10; and problem and target group, 11; and social science knowledge, 7-8; summary on, 16; testing and refining, 80-81; and unintended effects, 12; use of, 15-16

Projects: concept of, 24; in macrotheory, 98-99; means and structure at level of, 27

Public Law 94-142, 31

**Q**

Quality, and program philosophy, 21
Quay, H. C., 21, 41
Quick, S. K., 64, 76

**R**

Rabinowitz, V. C., 40
Radin, B., 77n
Ramsey, V. F., 76
Rayner, M., 100, 107
Reddy, M. J., 47, 57
Redman, E., 45, 57

Redner, R., 66, 76, 108
Reflection, as evaluation stage, 28, 30
Reilinger, E., 50, 56
Relationships, and conceptual heuristics, 48-49
Revelle, W., 19n, 32, 41
Rezmovic, E. L., 20, 21, 41, 42
Richardson, J., 51, 57
Roberts-Gray, C., 29, 39, 41
Rockart, J. F., 50, 57
Rog, D. J., 9, 11, 17-18, 77n, 78, 79, 92
Rogers, E. M., 70, 75
Roitman, D., 75, 76
Rokeach, M., 23, 42
Roos, L. R., Jr., 51, 57
Rosenblum, F., 72, 76
Ross, 14, 17
Rossi, P. H., 6, 7, 14, 17, 20, 21, 22, 40, 46, 57, 95, 96, 99, 105, 106, 107
Rothman, M. L., 37, 40, 41
Rubin, H. J., 101, 107
Rutman, L., 12, 18, 78, 92

**S**

Sabatier, P., 63, 76
Sabatino, D. A., 31, 42
Sanders, J. R., 20, 23, 42
Satow, R. L., 46, 57
Scanlon, J. W., 77, 78, 92, 95, 107, 108
Scheirer, C. J., 59n
Scheirer, M. A., 2, 5, 10, 11, 18, 20, 42, 50, 59, 61, 68, 71, 76
Schevers, T. J., 40
Schmidt, R. E., 78, 92
Schmitt, N., 75
Schneider, J., 76
Schön, D. A., 46, 47, 57
Scriven, M., 12, 16, 18, 94, 95, 96, 97, 100, 101, 102, 107-108
Sechler, E. S., 14, 16
Sechrest, L., 66, 76, 104, 108
Segal, S. P., 103, 108
Shadish, W. R., Jr., 2, 5-6, 7, 8, 16, 17, 21, 23, 24, 40, 46, 93, 95, 96, 97, 98, 99, 101, 102, 103, 104, 105, 106, 108, 109
Shaver, P., 95, 108
Shaklee, H., 14, 18
Shotland, R. L., 45, 57, 62, 76
Sims, D., 51, 52, 56
Smith, A. G., 68, 76

Smith, J. D., 82, 85, 92
Smith, J. K., 54, 57
Smith, J. M., 32, 41
Smith, M. L., 102, 108
Smith, N. L., 54, 57
*Smith* v. *Heckler*, 21
Social change: analysis of, 93–109; background on, 93–94; conclusion on, 104–105; difficulties of, 96–99; implementation of, 103–105; incremental, 99; short-term, 99–102
Social system: and implementation, 69–74; and program theory, 7–8
Staines, G., 95, 108
Stake, R. E., 6, 18, 19, 31, 42, 95, 96, 99, 108
Stakeholders: and consensus formation, 13; and implementation, 63, 65; and implicit theories, 14–15; multiple, 97
Stanley, J. C., 30, 40
Stein, L. I., 103, 108
Stobart, G., 17, 75
Stokey, A., 54, 57
Strauss, A. L., 90, 92
Stupak, R., 77n
Suchman, E. A., 10, 18, 97, 108

**T**

Tennessee, evaluability assessment of prenatal program in, 81–85, 90, 91
Test, M. A., 103, 108
Theory: concept of, 6, 60; and values, 23. *See also* Program theory
Tornatzky, L. G., 68, 70, 76
Toward Improving the Outcome of Pregnancy, 83–85
Trice, H. M., 68, 75
Trochim, W. M. K., 43n, 47, 57
Trumbull, D. J., 96, 108
Tuckman, B. W., 22, 23, 42
Tyler, R., 22, 42

**U**

Uncertainty, and formative evaluation, 44–46
Unintended effects, and program theory, 12
U.S. Department of Education, 78

U.S. Department of Health and Human Services, 78

**V**

Validity, construct of cause type of, 8
Values, and program philosophy, 22–23
Van de Ven, A. H., 44, 56
Veterans Administration, 42; Health Services Research and Development Service of, 36–39
Vogt, L. M., 108

**W**

Walker, D. F., 106
Walters, C., 19n
Watts, C. A., 41
Weatherley, R., 71, 76
Weick, K. E., 15, 18, 48, 53, 57
Weiner, S. S., 106
Weisbrod, B. A., 105, 108
Weiss, C. H., 10, 12, 18, 95, 96, 97, 99, 108
West, S. G., 108
Westinghouse Learning Corporation, 20, 30, 42
Wholey, J. S., 2, 5, 6, 12, 13, 14, 18, 19n, 21, 42, 77, 78, 79, 82, 83n, 85, 86, 87, 92, 95, 96, 97, 99, 107, 108
Wholey, M. S., 77n, 83n, 85, 92
Wicker, A. W., 44, 57
Wildavsky, A. B., 28, 41, 45, 57, 63, 68, 76, 95, 104, 105, 107
Williams, W., 63, 76, 104, 108
Windle, C., 101, 106–107
Work units, and implementation, 72
Worthen, B. R., 20, 23, 42
Wright, S. R., 46, 57

**Y**

Yeaton, W., 108
Yin, R. K., 64, 70, 76

**Z**

Zeckhauser, R., 54, 57